ABORN TO KWAITO

BORN TO KWAITO
Reflections on the kwaito generation

Esinako Ndabeni
&
Sihle Mthembu

BLACKBIRD
BOOKS

First published by BlackBird Books, an imprint of Jacana Media (Pty) Ltd, in 2018

10 Orange Street
Sunnyside
Auckland Park 2092
South Africa
+2711 628 3200
www.jacana.co.za

© Esinako Ndabeni & Sihle Mthembu, 2018
Images © Michael G Spafford, 2018

All rights reserved.

ISBN 978-1-928337-67-6

Cover design by Palesa Motsomi
Editing by Perfect Hlongwane
Proofreading by Linda Da Nova
Set in Minion Pro 11/15.5pt
Printed by ABC Press, Cape Town
Job no. 003294

See a complete list of BlackBird Books titles at www.jacana.co.za

To my grandmother, Thozama Notazi Thelma Ndabeni.
Ndibulela eza ntsomi wawundicela ukuba ndikubalisele, makhulu.
– Esinako Ndabeni

For Sne and Ntando
For Gogo and Ma
For Olwethu and Russel
And for Miss Kandai, I kept my promise.
– Sihle Mthembu

CONTENTS

Publisher's note ix

Acknowledgements xi

Politicising kwaito *Esinako Ndabeni* 1

Not 'South Africa's hip hop' *Esinako Ndabeni* 13

Mapaputsi makes it darker *Sihle Mthembu* 24

Plagued by hypermasculinity *Esinako Ndabeni* 41

Arthur Mafokate: Kwaito's most hideous man? *Sihle Mthembu* 50

Kwaito women *Esinako Ndabeni* 65

On kombuistaals and tsotsitaals *Esinako Ndabeni* 80

I wear what I like: Fashion and kwaito *Esinako Ndabeni* 93

TKZee: Amapantsul' ajabulile *Sihle Mthembu* 105

Yizo Yizo: The poetry of dysfunction *Sihle Mthembu* 118

The gangsta movie *Esinako Ndabeni* 137

Durban kwaito's future, past and present *Sihle Mthembu* . . . 150

Mandoza: Postscript for is'gelekeqe es'focused *Sihle Mthembu* 168

Producers paradise: A paean for the men on the boards
Sihle Mthembu.................................. 182

Looking back to the future *Esinako Ndabeni*........... 205

    About the authors 213

    References................................... 215

Publisher's Note

THE MOST BASIC DEFINITION of a book is that it is a written or printed work consisting of pages glued or sewn together along one side and bound in covers. As both a reader and a publisher, this description is far from my lived experience. As a reader, books to me are treasures. As a publisher, they are a legacy. This book is both.

Sihle first made contact with me in March of 2017 with a burden, an idea. The burdensome thing about ideas, especially exciting ones such as this one, is the fear that they may never come to fruition. As a publisher you then agonise, always for far too long – thinking about what could have been. Writing a book is a terrifying and daunting task, and it is for this reason that many great book ideas never come to see the light of day.

When I started BlackBird Books, one of the things I knew for sure was that we needed to create a platform for black people to begin, not to only unpack ourselves and our culture, but also to begin to interrogate the cultural impact that our lived experiences carry. Seeing this book come to life has felt like a beautiful reminder of that promise.

I cannot speak for any people outside of my generation, but kwaito feels like something that belongs to us, and there are not many things that we own completely. As a music genre, as a lifestyle, as a movement and as a culture, kwaito is ours – and this project feels like a step in the right direction for us as a generation

This book is not meant to be the definitive book and/or conversation on kwaito, but a reminder of a capsule in time. A nudge for us to do more, in terms of archiving the moments and the memories that continue to define us. It feels like a momentous step in the right direction, which will probably reverberate for a long time after we are gone.

To you, reader, I am extremely proud to bring you this offering. I am confident that this will not be the last you hear from both these authors, two of the most brilliant young minds I know. Esi and Sihle, I know the both of you had not bargained on the pressure that came with bringing this book to life, but you should be immensely proud. You can be sure that I am.

– Thabiso Mahlape, Polokwane 2018

Acknowledgements

INENE, UMNTU NGUMNTU NGABANTU. Stella Ndabeni-Abrahams; if I had to choose my own mother, I would still choose you. Thank you for giving me the freedom to be who I am. Sihle Mthembu; you have changed my life. Thabiso Mahlape; you embody Fierce. Please keep me around. I would like to thank the wonderful kwaito pioneers who entrusted us with their stories. Many people meet in this book. To name but a few: Perfect Hlongwane, Evelyn Nonqaba Ndabeni, Thato Abrahams, Kusisipho Abrahams, Somila Ngcongco, Chithibunga Ndabeni, Nyameka Mtirara, Phuti Marutla, Nthabiseng Mokitimi Dlamini, Lebohang Masango, Ana Deumert, Marlon Swai, Luvo Gila, Busisiwe Deyi, Precious Bikitsha, Nosipho Nwigbo, Lisa Vabaza, Njabulo Zwane, Thenjiwe Mswane, Sabelo Mcinziba, Miles Keylock, Charl Blignaut, Rhode Marshall, City Press, the UCT African Studies Book Collection, the National Library of South Africa…

'In my life, I've loved them all.'

– Esinako Ndabeni

1

Politicising kwaito
Esinako Ndabeni

To be black is to be burdened with the automatic, relentless work of saving other black people. A black person can't simply tell a story out of their love for stories – that story must carry with it some 'conscious' message, preferably political. At the very least, it is expected of black art that it should have the potential to offer solutions to the problems that we face. Of course, one can understand why these assumptions are often taken as given – black communities everywhere are beset with problems that need solving.

It's not surprising then that this same burden of responsibility was immediately imposed upon the kwaito generation; creating the oft-repeated narrative around the apparent 'meaninglessness' of kwaito. Former President Thabo Mbeki once famously referred to the genre as a 'distraction from real issues', echoing sentiments that were common among the political 'class' and older generations in South Africa's black communities.

It was to be expected that officialdom at that time would have frowned at black youths becoming apathetic or lackadaisical about issues of social reform in South Africa. The political rights that were attained post-1994 had not automatically ushered in socio-economic freedoms for the black majority who had borne the brunt of apartheid.

But this animosity towards kwaito; the insistence that it was a disengagement from the political, also revealed shortcomings in how the political was being re-imagined.

Dr Gibson Boloka's three-pronged definition of kwaito as: disengaging with socio-political discourse, breaking from previous traditions in black South African music, and a reflection of post-apartheid society, is not completely accurate. While kwaito clearly was a break from tradition and did reflect new cultural frames that emerged post-apartheid, I think it is important not to simply dismiss kwaito as apolitical. Perhaps kwaito would be better understood as having been driven in a sense by its own unique political nuances.

I intend to highlight the ways in which kwaito was not apolitical, and why it matters that we view the music as political text, but I also find it curious that black youths choosing to take a breather and seek pleasure through music is something that should have been perceived as so reactionary. It almost seems as if the youthful kwaito generation were begrudged their moment to be carefree; to live a little in the euphoria of the post-liberation relief that followed from apartheid's demise.

As someone born after the advent of kwaito, a 'born free' as we are often called, it's difficult for me to make older people understand why kwaito is so important to me. The older generations, who dismiss the genre even though they grooved to it when I was but a toddler, have clearly outgrown that phase. They now dismiss kwaito as the frivolous soundtrack of their youthful partying; little more than the background noise to which they socialised in the heady days of a newly liberated country. The enduring narrative seems to be that it was a genre by and for 'amavuilpop' (dirty hooligans). Nostalgia for kwaito's bygone appeal is often accompanied by an element of disdain.

But kwaito for me is the most important music genre and subculture that post-apartheid South Africa has birthed, and to see it leaving the collective memory, as it seems to be, without having witnessed a shift in how it is perceived, is disheartening. Even with the benefit of hindsight, kwaito is still branded as not having had any socio-political message to offer.

Lance Stehr, Managing Director of Ghetto Ruff, speaks passionately about this, highlighting what he believes to be the differences between, for example, pioneering South African hip hop outfit Prophets of da City's lyrical activism and the perceived indifference of kwaito music to 'real' issues. These are the insights Mr Stehr offers as we drive to Midrand from the Ghetto Ruff headquarters in Emmarentia:

> The reason why we only got into kwaito accidentally as a label was because we were into hip-hop before that. Now, with Prophets of da City for example, the point of doing music was to put out a political message because we were fighting against the government of the time. And kwaito, for me, was just a distraction. It didn't have a message at all. So, after the first democratic elections, all of a sudden nobody was interested in any socially conscious message. They were just into, 'Yeah, yeah let's party!' and we were like, 'What the fuck?' These songs had, like, two words the whole fucking song.

Engaging Mr Stehr, I try to get him to think about it from a different angle. 'Kwaito artists such as Oskido have said that it was a celebration of freedom,' I point out, but Mr Stehr sticks to his guns. 'Well, look where that freedom got us,' he scoffs. However, later on that same day, Mandla 'Spikiri' Mofokeng dismisses the idea that kwaito had no message.

'The problem with South Africans is that we don't believe in ourselves. We don't believe in our music. If Beyoncé can copy our dance moves then who are you to say that our home-grown kwaito has no meaning?' For Spikiri, kwaito is about identity; the expression of oneself and one's experiences through art forms such as fashion, dance and music.

I'm inclined to agree with Spikiri. It would be short-sighted of anyone not to understand that in a country where black expression had been severely policed, this unburdened expression of self was itself political.

That being said, there were some early kwaito acts whose lyrics explicitly verbalised their politics through the music. As freedom was dawning, acts such as Boom Shaka and Arthur Mafokate did not shy away from making overtly political music. With his song *Kaffir*, Mafokate openly challenged the derogatory terms and ideas that the descendants of the Dutch had attached to blackness ('Don't call me kaffir').

What interests me more, however, is Boom Shaka's rendition of the (then) black national anthem. For their album *It's Our Game (No Need To Claim)*, Boom Shaka chose to sing the national anthem over a house beat produced by DJ Christos. This rendition, with its unexpected synthesis of solemn lyrics with a danceable beat, encapsulated the nature of the kwaito generation's partying. It was partying, yes, but it was political. There was an awareness that did not necessarily need to be stated. Perhaps, to echo Gavin Steingo, the problem with our idea of the expressed politic is that we are more inclined to embrace politics that are explicitly stated. But politics are meant to be lived too, not just spoken.

Reading into the words unsaid

Bhekizizwe Peterson (citing Frith, 1996), cautions us against imagining that meaning is only made in lyrical content. Thinking deeply about Mshoza's use of the exclamation 'eish!' (oh!) in the song *Kortes*, Peterson goes on to show how even seemingly meaningless words have meaning. 'Eish!' in this instance speaks to how speechless Mshoza's crush made her when she saw him for the third time. What is not said past that point is all the things that we can imagine from her intonation of this seemingly empty word.

Of course, it's easy to arrive at this conclusion because we have the context of the lyrics before that point, which leads us to this understanding. Had the song merely said 'eish!' over a kwaito beat, I'm not quite sure it would have been as easy for Mr Peterson to make his argument. The point then is not that we ought to scramble to find deep meaning even when, for example, M'du Masilela says, 'Tsiki tsiki yho'; merely that it would help us to broaden how we understand expressions in their acquired contexts where kwaito is concerned.

The significance of language; the weight of words, is not something I want to argue against. In fact I remember a time when I disliked fine art because it did not come with verbal cues pointing to the meaning/s. It seemed to me that subtitles would make some works so much easier to appreciate/understand. Indeed, explicitly stated messages seem to have more impact upon first glance.

But over time I've grown to develop a sense that what is not explicitly stated, what is left unsaid, is often of great importance. Underlining this growing sense of the unreliability of words, we now have increased societal awareness that what is said is not always an accurate reflection of the artist and, perhaps then, even the art. We have reached the stage, at last, where we increasingly want the personal, the *private*, to be consistent with what the art and the artist espouse.

It is impossible for me now to listen to Brown Dash's *Vum Vum* without being conflicted by Brickz's verse on the song. Brickz tells the girl he's talking to in the song that, as imperfect as kwaito men are, he is not a 'skorobho' (a dirty person). I had always felt passionately about the song because on it Brown Dash, M'du and Brickz interrogate the respectability politics which tend to accompany responses to kwaito music.

This music emerged from the township. Kwaito artists prided themselves on the identity they'd formed from their township experiences, and I've always suspected that the sneering at kwaito betrays an implicit sneering at black youths from the township. On *Vum Vum,* M'du's verse challenges these ideas as he addresses kwaito's critics: 'Ningas'thathi kancane manis'bona sjampajampa emabheshen' emalok'shini' (Don't look down on us when you see us jumping around and dancing at bashes in the townships). Brickz follows along a similar vein as he reprimands a girl for 'judging a book by its cover'. *Words, words, words.* As I write this, Brickz has been convicted of raping his 16-year-old niece. It has become a struggle for me to reconcile his words with his actions. This is why it is important to disrupt the ways in which we think about political messaging; to realise that there is often more than meets the eye even when expression seems legit.

Of course, much of the kwaito generation did not take these projections to heart and burden themselves with the 'socially conscious' responsibilities that were being imposed upon them. They simply decided what they would and would not say and got on with it. This was itself a form of resistance, for to this day we live in a country where black expressions of self are often policed.

'Apartheid was over,' DJ Oskido says in the documentary *After Robot.* 'We just wanted to have fun as there would no longer be any need to protest.' How indeed could black youths not have shared in the excitement and grabbed at the chance to have a moment to breathe? After all, the very first black, democratically elected president, Nelson Rolihlahla Mandela had just sworn to them that, 'Never, never and never again shall it be that this beautiful land [would] again experience the oppression of one by another.' Merely 'having fun' really shouldn't have been seen as such a scandalous idea for the kwaito generation to embrace. However, I do believe it remains important for us to discuss just how politically relevant kwaito music was.

Kwaito as upward mobility

In particular, I would argue that the escape from material conditions of lack and the achieving of upward social mobility is a very understated aspect of the discourse around kwaito. This is probably because class positionality makes for an untidy account of the black South African experience. The fact that class is mostly determined by race in South Africa makes blackness the focal point of marginality in many ways. However, as we have witnessed more and more in post-apartheid South Africa, there are black folks who have formed an upper crust, and there is a real struggle around questions of how to engage with this emergent elite.

Kwaito is often understood in the context of poverty, which is fair. However, there has been little interrogation of how the music also became a tool for achieving upward social mobility, therefore positioning the genre as a means for many to escape poverty.

Even kwaito artists themselves grapple with this reality, at best, uncomfortably. This will become clearer in Sihle's chapter on Mandoza, where he talks about how Mandoza's music lost some of its resonance as his lyrical content became more removed from his 'real life' circumstances towards the end. As Sihle observes, Mandoza still imagined himself to be the underdog and could not quite fathom that he had 'made it'.

The reality is that, as much as life 'ekasi' (in the township) would always be a part of him, Mandoza's experience of and position in the world had changed; it was no longer only of the township and the material conditions of lack which accompanied this.

Going back to our meeting with Spikiri, I was quite astounded to notice the way in which his humility seemed to trickle into his consumption habits as well. Simply clad in black jeans, a t-shirt and his signature All Star sneakers, he remarked that the people he hung around with were not wealthy people, and he hated the thought of seeming as though he was somehow 'better' than them. I was almost embarrassed to be recording him on my iPhone 8 while he sat there with a Samsung model that I couldn't even recognise. He was adamant that although he had left the township, he had not abandoned it.

When I asked why he'd left, he chuckled and said that 'one could get no peace' in the township. His response left me with a keen sense of the struggle kwaito artists face between wanting to leave the township for all its socio-economic ills and still wanting to cling to what they imagine to be what Professor Adam Haupt labels 'the tyranny of authenticity'. In his paper, *Black masculinity and the tyranny of authenticity in South African popular culture*, Professor Haupt makes his analysis of this phenomenon of authenticity through the gangster movie, *Hijack Stories*. Sox, one of the two leading characters, wants to land the role of a gangster named Bra Biza on a TV show. However, as his family has moved up and out to Rosebank, Sox does not have the authenticity of the township figure. Professor Haupt writes about the 'authentic' role of the gangster that emerged in popular culture: Papa Action of *Yizo Yizo*, Panic Mokgotlane of *Mapantsula*, Bra Zama of *Hijack Stories*. Through this analysis of Sox's positioning as a middle-class figure, we start to see how 'inauthenticity' can create what my friend Lisa termed 'displacement dysmorphia' one night as we had energy drinks and dissected my romanticism of my rural home since moving into suburbia.

I say all of this to say that there is a complexity to the performance of the identity of the kwaito artist and the black South African. Spikiri's humility is something that seems to be imaginable only through his constant ties with the township – which grant him an authenticity. One thing is clear: the trajectory of the more focused and fortunate kwaito stars was always upward and headed towards suburbia.

Maybe the real difficulty lies in our processing of this concept of authenticity itself. Clearly the formation of insider and outsider categories is not something that is exclusive to systematically powerful groups. Powerlessness/underdog status can also become a social currency. As I write this essay, the discourse around oppression has become fashionable again and made its way back into pop culture.

As a pushback against this trend many young black feminists, for example, can be heard championing the view that 'the revolution' should be led by poor, black, disabled transwomen… I would however argue that these 'intersectionalities' also lead to performances around positionality. In any case, this is how poverty and dispossession is still the lens through which kwaito is viewed; because a currency has been attached to that identity.

I certainly would not like to claim that success exists only in the ways that capitalism has shaped, but I would still like to think that blackness need not always be defined by poverty. We have to get out. We have to break out of the cycle of generational poverty one way or another. And if, at any point, there had been a realisation that highlighted the class shift which the kwaito genre made possible for black youths at its peak, I don't think that engagement with the music and its subculture would have remained as simplistic as seems to be the case. Which is not to say that I was always aware of the complexity of the issues at play.

In the initial stages of my research into kwaito, for instance, I would often worry about whether I was encroaching by writing about a township experience which I do not have, as one who has only really moved between the village and the suburb. In this way, this project has also been eye-opening for me as a young black woman; for me to understand and position my own experiences better.

Engaging in conversations with artists such as Zola 7 and having him tell me that he, like me, had studied anthropology, helped me to (re)place myself and rethink some of the stereotypes I was bringing to my own process. Moments like these highlighted just how simplistic my engagement with the narrative around kwaito culture had been.

Kwaito culture created and provided many economic opportunities. It became a way to make a living across different disciplines. The street-wear label Loxion Kulca became fashionable and was championed by major kwaito acts such as Zola 7, TKZee and Mshoza. Record labels that would come to stand the test of time were founded on the back of kwaito's currency. The record label Kalawa Jazmee grew into an empire.

'It's like Coke,' Spikiri says, retelling his favorite analogy to Sihle and me. 'You then have Fanta, Sprite, and so on.' The Kalawa Jazmee record label, comprising of Oskido, Spikiri and Don Laka, has its foundations in the kwaito movement. It has become a versatile powerhouse which today houses a range of artists and keeps the spirit of kwaito alive. When Spikiri tells his story of being a keyboard player for Chicco Twala, and then deciding that he had to go and learn sound engineering, you cannot help but think that his success was well-planned. Methodical. With his musicality and roots in house music, Oskido has also managed to remain relevant artistically.

This record label, along with other black-founded record labels such as 999, TS Records and others, managed to use kwaito music as a way to build a future for themselves, and now these ghetto jams are produced in suburbia. Kwaito enabled artists to venture into television: Zola 7's TV show titled *Zola 7* and Kabelo Mabalane's *Play Your Part* were by-products of the success of kwaito.

Kwaito in campaign politics

While doing research for this book, Sihle and I stumbled upon a 1999 African National Congress (ANC) election advertisement that left us speechless with confusion. 'Kwaito today, but without your vote the future is jungle,' it read. It was the kind of cryptic assertion that Chazz could have been referring to on *Blades of Glory*: 'No one knows what it means but it's provocative; it gets the people going'.

This election poster was a reinforcing of the view that kwaito was at best a short-sighted genre (the future is jungle). I think that perhaps this kind of thinking was also a reflection of the time, which is to say before the realisation that freedom is always shifting its goalposts.

Even the very politically conscious hip hop outfit Prophets of da City took a moment to celebrate what most South Africans imagined to be an irreversible victory. The first verse on their 1994 hit song *Never Again* begins with Shaheen Ariefdien exclaiming, 'ah, excellent! Finally a black president'. This relief, this sense of euphoria even from a group that was decidedly hyper-political, suggests that the mood of short-sighted celebration was not unique to the kwaito acts of the time.

Kwaito artists did eventually become closely involved in party politics. When political parties started recognising the value of engaging the youth (votes), they began to forge alliances with kwaito artists. In 2002, the former Deputy Minister of Arts, Culture, Science and Technology, Brigitte Mabandla, announced that the ANC would 'be engaging kwaito musicians to explore how [they] could enable the growth of kwaito as well as examine its potential in the socio-economic development of our country'.

The kwaito generation had become a force to be reckoned with and its influence in society was being acknowledged in officialdom. Trompies star turned political activist Eugene Mthethwa and Arthur Mafokate were at the forefront of the engagement with party politics. Both were known for being at the forefront of doing ANC promotional work in the 2009 elections. Mthethwa used his influence to become the secretary general of the Creative Workers Union of SA: a union affiliated with the Congress of South African Trade Unions (Cosatu), and also managed the Presidential Hotline established in 2009. Mafokate publicly endorsed the ANC in order to garner support for the party from the kwaito-loving youth. Recently, he has also been involved in campaigning for the Democratic Alliance.

A mo(ve)ment in time

Today kwaito is mostly played in shebeens by people who want to have fun times and perhaps momentarily forget the daily struggles of their lives. With its origins in house music, it covertly flirts with politics sometimes, but mostly chooses to be the kind of music that can be enjoyed with a beer or a cider in low-pressure situations.

When one considers the political significance of black people deciding to take a moment to enjoy themselves, these choices cannot be characterised as simply 'apolitical'. When one chooses to be joyful in the moment (where one's joy is often perceived as immaterial or even sinister), this joy becomes a politically significant gesture. We should make space for this while acknowledge all the explicitly political content that has been discussed in kwaito ranging from flagging domestic violence to activist messaging against the spread of HIV/AIDS.

The kwaito moment represents celebration for a generation that has nonetheless shaped much of its identity on reclamation and contestation. When Arthur Mafokate threw the word 'kaffir' around more times than many would have liked in his iconic song, the nonchalant repetition of the word was at the same time undercutting the power of this derogatory term on the lips of those who weaponised it against black people. This was a moment that captured the freedom that the younger generations were embracing. Not only was 'generation kwaito' dancing and carefree, it was also laughing in the face of oppression; undermining a history scarred with pain that sought to stifle their newfound right to unbridled expression. If it is not clear and still needs to be spelt out: kwaito was a political mo(ve)ment.

II

Not 'South Africa's hip hop'
Esinako Ndabeni

A FRIEND OF MINE WHO WAS starting a hip hop magazine once asked me to join as a 'kwaito writer' since, 'hip hop is kwaito anyway'. Upset, I told my best friend about this request. Why does everyone think that Kwaito is hip hop's stepchild? It turned out that my bestie didn't share my indignation. I launched into a passionate monologue about why kwaito is not hip hop. 'No, the fact that Zola 7 raps in isiZulu does not mean that kwaito is a derivative of hip hop, it is a lot more complicated than that,' I implored. Granted, the kwaito/hip hop debate has been raging for almost as long as kwaito itself has been alive. Memorably, the iconic and now defunct *Y Magazine* had readers who would often write in to express the view that kwaito music was 'a disgrace to hip hop'.

But rap, even at its most elementary, is something I believe comes naturally to African people. Even our history at base is oral and poetic. To hear African artists speaking over a beat should not automatically be equated with hip hop culture or copycat attempts at rapping. Senyaka, who credits himself as one of the pioneers of the kwaito genre (there's no doubt that he was there at the very beginning), explains in the documentary *After Robot: Kwaito Music in Johannesburg* that his rapping (over the synth-heavy disco beats which South Africans called 'bubblegum' in the 1980s), came from a place of wanting to express himself so people could understand him. Except Senyaka Kekana didn't have a singing voice, so he opted to speak over the beats in order to express himself.

In Senyaka's case, through cutting-edge hits like *Go Away*, we can hear that his rap-like vocals came to him instinctively, confirming that spoken words in a musical setting were something that existed in our diffuse African cultures before and outside of hip hop. Of course it's possible that these artists had heard some early hip hop because even before the turn of the century the planet was already a global village, with global citizens able to consume music from all parts of the world. In fact, Spikiri says the iconic rapper Snoop Dogg was one of his musical influences.

Cultural exchange is inevitable when we engage with other societies. However, it is also very clear to me that kwaito was rooted in an entirely different sound from hip hop. Later on, overlap may have deepened as acts such as Zola 7, Mzambiya and Mshoza emerged, introducing rap-like lyrics in vernacular languages to the genre. But the sound was not, to my mind, rooted in hip hop.

The house music connection

On May 22 2016 Oskido uploaded a video on Instagram with the caption: 'Many people don't know the source; when making kwaito I was inspired by this song. From here we created a kwaito movement.' In the background, Nightcrawler's *Push The Feeling On* was playing: a house record. This is not a statement one can ignore, coming as it does from one of the founding fathers of kwaito. But in researching material for this book, I've come to the conclusion

NOT 'SOUTH AFRICA'S HIP HOP'

that there is a much wider variety of influences on kwaito music to be unearthed, well beyond the popular and lazy tendency to characterise the music as primarily a by-product of hip hop, house and bubblegum.

Some of the problems relating to how hip hop is framed are mainly problems that my particular generation grapples with. My best friend, Nosipho, and I struggle to agree on the defining criteria of blackness when we talk about music. I have always been resistant to centering the African-American story in South African narratives of resistance. I believe that marginality doesn't mean total powerlessness, and that western imperialism can also manifest itself in the predominance of resistance art by oppressed peoples from superpower countries.

There's an undeniable amplifying of the African-American voice that is afforded by the scale of black art industries in the US that we simply do not have here at home. So I've always made a conscious effort to ensure that I relate to the various art forms in ways that foreground our homegrown art forms which are often overrun when we use the global lens without checking ourselves.

Nosi, on the other hand, relates better to African-American artists than to South African influences. But I realise that my friend is authentic and passionate in championing the liberation of black people despite our differences. Engaging with globalisation and creating a very personal politic from a context wherein one is in some senses an 'outsider', is a contradiction that black youths in the global south grapple with every day.

For me the fixation that we seem to have with finding, 'the South African equivalent of anything that is American' is discomfiting. In many ways it speaks to the one-sided cultural exchange that we young South Africans find ourselves having with American pop culture. Perhaps rapper Cassper Nyovest articulated my reservations best in his 2017 interview with the American hip hop themed *Breakfast Club*. Following questions about which act from the United States he could best be compared to, he said:

Where I'm from, we often compare. When you say, you know, who am I like... When you compare in terms of how big I am, it's like a compliment. When people say 'Yo, you're like, the Kanye of South Africa'... It's how we think, you know. My whole thing is to change that. I just wanna be Cassper Nyovest of the world.

Globalisation and its benefits, including the freer movement of art, has nonetheless privileged the culture of the more ascendant West. A simple example of this is that it's much easier and more likely that one will be exposed to American hip hop music in South Africa, than it is that one would encounter kwaito while living in the US. One result of this is that it has become increasingly difficult to identify South African cultural icons who haven't assimilated into western culture.

The big 'very authentically African' South African artists who are referenced are often older acts such as Ladysmith Black Mambazo, Caiphus Semenya and so on. This is not to suggest that these legendary acts had no outside influences; merely to state just how much the external has influenced South African music more recently. This can hardly be said to have begun only post-1994, however, it is commonly acknowledged that South Africa's bubblegum music of the eighties was a localised variation of disco music.

It does however seem to me that the increasing dominance of hip hop has bred a different kind of identity politic. For instance, young South Africans today find themselves animatedly discussing why white people should not be allowed to say the word 'nigga', as if white people in South Africa walk around using American slurs and slang. That said, the South African assimilation and adoption of hip hop music hasn't been without contestation.

The space for hip hop in South Africa's popular culture

I will admit to having been one of the people who advocated, perhaps too one-sidedly, for local music with an imperfect understanding of how the local is made. I prided myself in staying true to what is African and, more specifically, South African. This is the place from where my love for kwaito had been ignited. The late, great Busi Mhlongo also became one of my favourite South African artists as I went through the TIDAL streaming app's archives, looking for pieces of myself I could recognise in the music.

Although it first surprised me when I discovered that mam' Busi had lived for a long time in Portugal and London, on her album *Urban Zulu* I began to catch the aroma of a culturally diverse brew. In that album, she had recorded the song *Oxamu* – originally recorded by Mama Miriam Makeba. At her concert at the Market Theatre with the late and great force, utata uJabu Khanyile, uMam' uBusi would do a reggae rendition of the song. And as she did this, she crooned with the instinctive spirituality of the black South African. She was able, it dawned on me, to merge different experiences to create her own undeniably African interpretation. Around this time I also began to think very deeply about my disdain for local hip hop.

The African-American author Yvonne Bynoe boldly proclaims that, 'while rap music has been globalised, hip hop music has not been and cannot be'. In her article titled *Getting Real About Global Hip Hop*, Bynoe questions the extent to which rap music made by black artists outside of the USA can form part of hip hop culture. This is premised on her assertion that if culture is shaped by history and traditions, it is almost impossible for those who do not share this history or partake in its traditions to make claims to said culture. Hip hop as a culture goes beyond the music, she says, and even further beyond its components of MCing, B-Boying, Aerosol art (graffiti); it is a culture intricately embedded within a unique history.

This would mean that even if South African artists perfected the art forms that form part of hip hop culture, their identity as South African would hinder them from becoming fully integrated into the hip hop tradition. Even before I came across Bynoe's ideas, I had felt that South African hip hop communicated a disconnect with the local identity and was reaching out to a culture in which it would never achieve 'insider' status. This was an unnecessary problem, I felt then, which local musos would not face if they stuck to kwaito, because it was centered in their own black South African experience.

Having researched and thought about these issues in the course of this book's writing life, I can safely say I no longer have the vehement rejection of local hip hop that I had before. I've grown more aware and open to the fact that the world is a place of interaction and cultural exchange, and that we are privileged today with the ability to mirror and be mirrored across different cultures and traditions. However, while I do believe that Bynoe's argument has its limitations, I also still believe that it should compel us to seek to champion a culture that is rooted in our own experiences as South Africans. This is why I believe that it will always be important for kwaito to live on in our discourse.

Something borrowed

One of my anthropology lecturers' favourite stories was Amos Tutuola's *The Palm-Wine Drinkard*. In his course titled *The Challenge of Culture*, Professor Nyamnjoh was bent on helping us understand mobility and culture. He taught us about the interest in understanding the movements of cultures; for example, the fact that one could say they were studying Cape Town's Khayelitsha township but miss the fact that a portion of the township leaves for the city every morning around 5am and returns in the evening. So, the township continually moves into and out of the inner city and the suburbs. The idea is clear: culture is not static, and we ought to broaden our understanding of where we imagine different cultures are located and how they live and breathe.

The Palm-Wine Drinkard tells the story of a spoilt young man who enjoys palm wine so much that he has his own man preparing the palm wine for him: a tapster. When this man dies, the young man is unwilling to accept it so he travels to Dead's Town in an attempt to bring him back. On this journey, he falls in love with a young woman and marries her. However, as he goes through this magical Dead's Town he encounters a few misadventures. Luckily, he has *juju* (magical power) that lets him shift into different forms to help him outwit his foes.

Professor Nyamnjoh's analysis of this, as seen in his paper *Incompleteness: Frontier Africa and the Currency of Conviviality*, is that we can only dream of completeness if we have borrowed elsewhere. In all his shapeshifting, the palm-wine drinker has to shift back after he is finished. 'Being and becoming as works in progress,' Professor Nyamnjoh writes, 'require borrowings and enhancements to render them beautiful and acceptable.'

While he writes in a different context, I believe that this is an important takeaway for our engagement with cultures 'outside' our own. The sound of home can be informed by a collaboration with influences from outside of home. Professor Nyamnjoh goes on to say that, 'Bodies and forms are never complete; they are open-ended, malleable vessels to be appropriated by consciousness in its multiplicity'. These insights add to my understanding that 'borrowings and enhancements' from the outside do not diminish the value of the localised work that kwaito artists have done.

Chiskop, the famous group that consisted of Mduduzi 'Mandoza' Tshabalala, Siphiwe 'The General GTZ' Sibisi, Sizwe 'Lollipop' Motaung and Sibusiso 'Bless' Thenjekwayo, displayed the richness that can result from borrowing from other cultures. With their love for breakdancing, the group incorporated breakdance in their pantsula-infused stage performances, and were unique because of it. Even streetwear label Loxion Kulca was founded by young men who had a profound love for hip hop (and played for the Wits University basketball team in the mid-nineties), but who also took great pride in their identity as young black South Africans. In dress sense and style, from the popular Chuck Taylor sneakers to Lebo Mathosa and Brenda Fassie's famous updo braided hairstyles, it was clear that South African kwaito artists borrowed considerably from images consumed via [African] American film.

My problem with some aspects of the kwaito versus hip hop debate, beyond the culturally imperialistic undertones in it, is the fact that it is an inaccurate narrative. The pioneers of kwaito music have never been secretive about the artistic influences that they drew from to create the sound. Arthur Mafokate states explicitly in the doccie *After Robot: Kwaito Music in Johannesburg* that kwaito music was 'a slowed down disco music'. Others, such as Brothers of Peace and DJ Oskido, point out that kwaito music was heavily influenced by house music.

The first kwaito song to break into post-apartheid South African radio was Arthur Mafokate's title song from his EP titled *Kaffir*. Released in 1995, the title song's beat is disco, only it is twice as slow. Addressing a Boere baas, Mafokate antagonistically repeats, 'Hey, baas, don't call me kaffir' while Queen sings the chorus melodiously in the background. Lyrically, this song captured the newfound freedom that South Africans felt when apartheid was outlawed, but Mafokate's repeated, nonchalant use of the word 'kaffir' would come to symbolise the problem that many had with kwaito music as a symbol of immorality.

The early kwaito pioneers were cognisant of the fact that they could not merely make slowed down disco or house music without incorporating elements of South African culture which would set them apart. Brothers of Peace were particularly adept at this, infusing elements of maskandi music into their house beats to make their own version of kwaito. Songs like *eGoli Gauteng* came to encompass the South African story of rural-to-urban migration, with Mageu singing, in his evocative gravel voice, 'bang'shay' eGoli' (they beat me in Johannesburg), in a way that can only be done by drunk black men from the rural areas. A more striking example is their song *Meropa (Pitseng tse kgolo)*, where BOP sampled Mahlathini and the Mahotella Queens and drew from the traditional mgqashiyo beat.

Similarly, Brenda Fassie's kwaito album *iMali* is reminiscent of many of the folk songs sung by Xhosa people. While disco is an undeniable aspect of the sound, it also comes out clearly that these artists had done the work of understanding the uniqueness of their identities and the audiences with which they were communicating. Professor in Sociology Sharlene Swartz once described the sonics of kwaito music as, 'a raucus beat, a mix of slowed down house with African urban rhythms and sounds literally sampled into the mix'.

Frankly, for all the English that I have at my disposal, I still struggle to describe music. It is something that is felt more than it is heard. I have yet to learn how to translate the feeling of a song into a language we can all speak. On his blog, *Working Class Celebrity*, writer and lead singer of the band The Muffinz, Sfiso Atomza, says that, 'kwaito was groove music, tavern music, "let the good times roll" music'. And that is just it. To me, kwaito sounds like a dark room with everybody holding a Black Label dumpie or a bottle of Savannah as they do the get-down.

Of course, some kwaito artists grew to fall outside of and expanded our ideas about kwaito music as simply slowed down disco or house music with samples of black urban rhythms. The legendary group TKZee for example, had a different approach. While many artists were more focused on studio engineered and sample-laced kwaito, TKZee chose the route of incorporating classical music and real musical instruments into the genre. Zwai Bala, who had studied classical music with the world famous Drakensburg Boys Choir, and Tokollo and Kabelo, who interestingly met in high school at the highbrow St Stithians High in Jo'burg, brought new elements into a genre that was already quite diffuse.

TKZee would go on to collaborate with the late, great jazz maestro, Moses Taiwa Molelekwa. By such unlikely routes did the band arrive at making kwaito music with live instruments, as opposed to mainly studio equipment, as was the norm within the genre.

A major distinction for me between kwaito and hip hop is that the former symbolised a post-apartheid elation. The illusions of the emerging rainbow nation were dominating the way that many of these artists saw the world. Excited by the promise of an equal post-apartheid South Africa, kwaito artists looked to this 'let the good times roll' sound as a moment to breathe a sigh of sweet relief and to, well, let the good times roll. We see, in Mdu and Mzekezeke's music videos for example, white women making cameo appearances: proof that there was an imagining and an embracing of a South Africa that had moved towards racial integration of all the colours of the rainbow.

Hip hop's emergence on the other hand was rooted in protest: Afrika Bambaataa's Universal Zulu Nation, one of the earliest fully-fledged hip hop outfits, was concerned with spreading social awareness. Perhaps this can also be used to highlight some distinctions between kwaito and later resurgences of South African hip hop; the fact that the latter came to the fore as the honeymoon era in South African society began to show its cracks, during the later stages of kwaito's reign.

And there was little confusion about it. Pro Kid's debut album *Heads and Tails* was released in the same year as the Brothers of Peace's album *King of Kwaito Uyagawula*. The lines between the two genres were clear; one was hip hop and the other was kwaito.

Identity is fluid. In the age of the internet, it is almost impossible to define ourselves as strictly black South Africans, because our lives have now been woven into global experiences. So I have no desire to be an African purist: I sincerely believe that societies need to normalise borrowing from other cultures and abandon the idea that a culture is only legitimate if it is entirely homegrown.

However, I am also strongly advocating for the understanding of our local contexts and identities. It is important that our stories not get lost in the consuming pit of cultural imperialism.

It would help us to centre ourselves in our narratives without feeling the need to draw comparisons to overarching western or global cultures. Things may be changing because of hip hop's dominance on the current popular South African music scene, but South Africa's interaction with western, largely American culture, has generally tended to be one of reverence even while appropriating it. While parallels certainly can be drawn between different cultures, the fact that there is this desperation to frame kwaito as 'South African hip hop', or South Africa's equivalent of any other western parallel, is telling of the dominance that the West's media and culture has in our country. It suggests (wrongly) that we can only legitimately create, recreate and understand ourselves through the lenses of the western experience.

III

Mapaputsi makes it darker
Sihle Mthembu

Last July I signed a book deal to write a collection of essays about the music of kwaito. For a while I was ecstatic. The picture of me signing the publishing contract, sitting on the red chairs in my office boardroom, is still one of my favourite things. I'd been working towards this moment for 15 years; ever since my 5th Grade English teacher Miss Kandai had read to us *The Adventures Of Tom Sawyer*, and I'd told her that I would be an author one day. This was me keeping my promise. For a while everything seemed bright and bearable. A memory kept replaying itself repeatedly in my mind; that moment after Kevin Garnett and the Boston Celtics had just clinched the 2008 NBA championship. When a journalist asked Garnett how he felt, he screamed, 'Anything is posssssssssiiiiibllleee!'

I usually write at night, so by the time summer came around and I was deep in the trenches of doing the work, the writing days got shorter. I began to feel irritable and ill. The motivation of a dream coming true no longer fueled my desire to plough through mounds of research to make sense of the songs and the memories.

To sit at my laptop for hours and articulate what I had felt, what we had lost, began to feel less like a privilege and more like a burden. In those months, I found a steady and welcome stream of distractions, ranging from watching reaction videos on YouTube, to binge-reading twitter threads that seemed improbable but entertaining. Or making endless and ultimately useless lists like Quentin Tarantino's films ranked from best to worst:

1. *Inglorious Basterds*
2. *Pulp Fiction*
3. *Jackie Brown*
4. *Kill Bill vol 1*
5. *Reservoir Dogs*
6. *Kill Bill vol 2*
7. *Django Unchained*
8. *The Hateful Eight*
9. *Death Proof*

I used all these activities as a deflection from dealing with whatever blockage was preventing me from writing; anything to avoid writing the stories I had so longed to pour of out of my self and onto the page. As the days merged into weeks, the anxiety of having a task with no allocated start date began to take its toll. I transitioned from telling myself that I was merely thinking about the work, to hating myself for being lazy.

My publisher, Thabiso Mahlape, and co-author checked in from time to time but they were not overbearing, and I was grateful for that. My friends and my partner would ask how things were going. It was clear to me that there was no rational way to explain that I was waking up religiously at 3am, but by the time I had to get ready for work at 6am I'd barely strung together a paragraph. Let me say right now that I don't believe in writer's block. I have written on train rides and in the middle of fights and protests. Also, during the time of this siege, and that is what I call it, a siege, I was still able to write other things. In fact I penned some of my most cherished journalistic work during this dark period.

Even reading, which since I was a boy had always been a welcome outlet and a source of relief and inspiration, seemed to become nothing more than a bottomless fountain of anxiety. Every book and essay I read felt like a personal attack; a confirmation that I was a fraud who would never be able to write something significant. I had worshipped books all my life and I wanted to write one as a way of giving to others what had been given to me. Yet here I was feeling delirious and never more alone. On the days when I lay on my bed fantasising about calling Thabiso and telling her to call the whole thing off, I felt like I was on the brink of betraying a lover who had plucked me out of the terror of my youth. I knew I had to go on; the real work was finding out how.

Maybe, I speculated, it was seeing all my peers seemingly free and happy in their lives in a way that had seemed to elude me for years. Maybe that was what I couldn't get out of my head. Maybe it was the amount of money that I didn't have but so desperately wanted. Or perhaps it was a result of the bad grammar that came with having been educated at a public school during South Africa's transition in and out of the OBE system. There was also the possibility that all of this was coupled with the anxiety of being a father and soon-to-be-husband, converging to create a recipe that made writing not just difficult but practically impossible.

Back then I still held on to the fantasy of the writer needing to get away from their own life in order to write. But if you are outside of your lived experience what could you possibly have to write about, and why would anyone care? 'I use my own experiences because my own experiences are the only thing I have available to me,' says the writer Mike Nichols. It became obvious to me that to isolate myself was not the way to write about kwaito. That in order to have words on the page, I would need to spend less time at my computer trying to get water from a stone, and go out into the world.

So one December evening during a cold visit to Jo'burg, where I was viewing the third and final cut of a sci-fi short film I'd directed, I decided to make my way to Bekkersdal, to a small tavern called Big Fish. I almost immediately regretted doing this though, because the two hour drive to this place was no fun. I had convinced a friend who I hadn't seen in years, and who in fact was not really my friend but my best friend's brother, to come with me. He brought his girlfriend along, and I was grateful that they had each other to talk to so I wouldn't be tasked with filling the silence with small talk.

They picked me up from the once-posh suburb of Auckland Park, and we began to make our way to one of the more remote townships in Gauteng. The type of place you never hear anything good or bad about, but see below as you fly out and think, 'People are living there'.

For a cover charge of R50 we would get to see Jakarumba, whom I had always felt was underrated as a songwriter and solo act, Alaska (which was now a duo) and this other guy you might have heard about, Mapaputsi.

As a child, I knew Mapaputsi's voice before I knew his face. I imagined that now, with the right combination of age and cigarettes, he'd have grown to have a voice that sounded like a big brassy instrument; something like Louis Armstrong's. I first encountered Mapaputsi through his breakout single *Izinja*, which seemed to come out of nowhere into the light. Later on I would become even more familiar with him, via a very rundown bootleg tape of the debut album with *Izinja*, which I got from my friend Thulani Nxele in 7th grade.

About a year later I would mistakenly tape over the cassette and record an Ukhozi FM Top 20 chart show that featured Young Buck's *Let Me In*, and this error would be one of the defining musical tragedies of my young life. For years after that, I searched for *Izinja* in vain.

Mapaputsi had always been a subject of fascination for me because, despite his notoriety and credentials as a hitmaker, he had somehow remained something of an enigma. At no point was he ever overexposed on TV like many of his peers, and he never really got big endorsement deals or magazine covers, except that one time he was on the cover of *Y Magazine* with Kabelo and Tshidi from Malaika. Even then, at the height of his fame, he came across as the kind of guy who was just happy to be around; who would always be alright simply because of how he navigated the murky waters of the music industry. This skill: the ability to retain the common touch and not get lost in the hype, often comes in very handy in the cutthroat game of music.

Over the years I've returned to *Izinja* habitually. I would survey its grungy cover, where an image of Mapaputsi takes up about two thirds of the cover frame, and there is this large target that almost threatens to obscure his face. Around him are signs that read, 'Beware of the dog'. Seeing an artist play so openly with perceptions about the inherent fear that is generated by the mere fact of ones existence as a black man made me giddy. The plots in the songs became familiar; stories about toxic friendships, expired love and attempts at happiness. Every time I listened to the album it was a reminder of home.

On this particular night in Bekkersdal, Mapaputsi wore a black shirt, some dark blue jeans and black shoes. He performed right at the end of the night, which had taken the format of a battle between old-school house and old-school kwaito. It was pretty clear from Alaska's opening performance, and settled beyond doubt by the time they got to *Accuse,* that kwaito would run away with the night. When Mapaputsi took to the stage the crowd was already electric. Older men and women, who had been sitting or getting drinks during the final house set, suddenly found themselves jostling for space in the front row with younger revellers who had money to spend and nostalgia to indulge. It was a small stage with barely any lighting, but the sound which came from eight large speakers fitted around the venue was surprisingly crisp.

Mapaputsi has this thing of performing with two mics and

switching between the two throughout his set. As he delivered a 45-minute set that was full of gusto and energy, the time seemed to just breeze by. He unleashed his signature hits, from *Lisa* and *My Love* to *Izinja* and *Woza Friday*, and by the time he got to *Kleva*, inserting several jazzy breakdowns in the groove, I was reminded why I had admired this man for so long, albeit from a distance. He was one of the beautiful ones; a not-so-problematic fave and a consummate professional. This was the second coming of Mapaputsi, and there was life in the old dog yet.

Rise and fall

Here are some things you might not know about Sandile Ngwenya aka Mapaputsi. He is an avid reader and a big fan of Mark Twain, or at least Mark Twain quotes. He loves stand-up comedy and frequents comedy shows every chance he gets. Mapaputsi got the name that became his stage moniker from an Italian shoe salesman who used to work in Zola. 'Paputsi' derives from an Italian dialect's word for shoes.

Mapaputsi has a deep love for animals, especially dogs. Since the time of *Izinja*, they have also become a recurring avatar in his work, gracing his single and album covers. In fact, he loves dogs so much they are the reason he volunteered to become an ambassador for an anti-animal cruelty campaign. Being with his dog relaxes him, he tells me, observing that it's certainly much better than being with humans. 'Animals are not as cruel as human beings I think. The things we do to hurt each other sometimes are just too much. Dogs have good spirits and if you keep them happy they don't ask for much,' he says.

He also loves smoking. A lot. Cigarettes, and weed. When I bring up the time he was almost arrested at Sun City during the 2003 SAMAs for smoking a joint, he laughs me out of the room.

'It was no big deal man, I was just surprised that the papers made such a big thing out of it because I still performed after that. I was high as a kite though, but I still remember it very well.' Mapaputsi says he's been trying to quit smoking all his life without success. It's a habit he picked up as a young boy growing up in Zola. During those years he also picked up a distinct love of music. 'I've always been a person that soaks up influence. When we were growing up smoking was something that everyone did and the smokes were even advertised. It's the same with music. I always say I never went to music, music came to me.'

Mapaputsi was a high school soccer prodigy, but he abandoned the sport to follow his love for music. By the time I became obsessed with *Izinja* in 2004, Mapaputsi had already released three hit albums back to back, and was regularly selling out shows and clubs around the country. His career had been made by *Izinja*, a thinly disguised homage or appropriation of Baha Men's *Who Let The Dogs Out?* The record went triple platinum and propelled him from proverbial insider-outsider to fully fledged superstar. Of the album he says:

> What people don't understand about that song is that it's not just about dogs barking, but it's also about freedom. It's about when we got the right to vote and were able to express ourselves, and that there was nothing that could hold us back. The dogs were out and anybody who wanted to hold us back would regret that.

But before all that 'barking', Mapaputsi had begun his musical journey with gospel. Raised in a conservative Christian family, Mapaputsi had started off by singing in choirs. In the early 1990s he got his big break when he was invited to write some material and record with Rebecca Malope and Pure Magic. He appears on *Somlandela*. Mapaputsi says this was the sign he needed to know that he wanted to do music full time. 'I didn't start with kwaito because what I fell in love with was music. I love to relay messages through music and singing, and that came out when I got into kwaito, because a lot of kwaito music I made was very harmonic.'

Around the same time Mapaputsi became active on the Zola kwaito scene as it was gaining momentum. However, he fancied himself as more of a songwriter and producer than a performer and regularly collaborated on songs with TKZee and Chiskop. 'These were guys I knew from hanging out ekasi and through mutual friends. They were musicians but they also didn't act like celebrities, and that's why for a lot of us that friendship remains because it was based on things more than money and even music. It was our shared identity.'

Producer Gabi le Roux says he recalls Mapaputsi always being around at Chiskop recording sessions and that Mapaputsi once gave him a demo which he didn't listen to 'until it was too late'.

I remember he'd always said we should make some music together and we planned to. One day he gave me this demo and I just never got around to listening to it because I was so busy all the time. The next thing I knew, I was hearing this guy on the radio, and even though I'd known he had talent, he sounded just phenomenal. I was a bit jealous that I didn't get around to producing for him before that.

Random acts of kindness seem to be the glue that hold Mapaputsi's career in place. In 2001 the popular YFM DJ Khabzela, who was one of Mapaputsi's best friends, encouraged him to start recording. Mavusana and Mizchif featured him on their *Summertime* project because he just happened to be in the studio when they were working on it. And through that chance collaboration, Mavusana introduced Mapaputsi to a then a relatively unknown producer by the name of D-rex. D-rex recalls meeting Mapaputsi and not being sure what to make of the man. 'He was just there in the studio one day and I just loved the tone of his voice. It wasn't like anything I'd heard or worked with before. Then I found out that he could actually write and knew a lot about structuring a song.'

Mapaputsi would go on to spend days and nights listening to drafts of music that D-rex had made and on some nights slept on the couch in the studio. D-rex would wake up to his day job of making adverts and Mapaputsi would focus on writing lyrics during the day, come back at night, and they would start laying down tracks. Reflecting on that time, Mapaputsi tells me he doesn't know how he had the energy to sustain that level of focus. 'There was definitely a lot of chemistry between us because I think we didn't like the repetitive structure of a lot of kwaito songs. D-rex had a lot of other music references like EDM and rock so our musical conversation became wider, and that was something that challenged and kept me on my toes as a musician.'

There is some debate around the origins of the opening line of *Izinja*, 'Aboban abakhumul' izinja la?' This lyric's genius was in appropriating the hit Baha Men single and then adding a distinct, colloquial township flavour to it. Brickz, who was and still is very close friends with Mapaputsi, was working closely with him at the time and contends that he wrote the line originally as, 'Aboban abakhumul' amabhubesi la?' Mapaputsi remembers things another way. 'It was just something that I always said and I remember going into the studio and laying it down and when D-rex added those dog-bark sound effects it was like an earthquake!'

I ask D-rex about the origins of the line. He pauses to think, lifting his eyes for a second before he answers. He tells me he isn't sure who came up with the opening line, but he is sure about who penned the verses. 'I can't really say either way but I do know for a fact that Mapaputsi wrote the verses for *Izinja* because he wrote them in front of me and it was so quick. I was still playing around with the melody and he already had them.'

On the strength of the music that come out of those sessions, Mapaputsi signed with Ghetto Ruff, in a deal which label exec Lance Stehr insists was hugely favourable to Mapaputsi. 'I knew that this was gold. There were no two ways about it. Mapaputsi was pure talent and we had to support him to get the music to go as far as it could.'

According to D-rex there is a funny little story about how Oskido reacted when he first heard *Izinja*. 'I can't remember who it was but someone once told me that Oscar was in the studio at YFM when the song came on and he took off his hat and said, 'This is the greatest song I've ever heard', and promptly stormed out of the building.'

The record flew off the shelves and earned Mapaputsi wins for Best Kwaito Artist and Best Kwaito Song at the Metro FM Awards in 2002. 'I think people found that record intriguing because it was very musical but kept the energy of the streets. It didn't feel forced in any way,' Mapaputsi says.

But even in those early days Lance Stehr recalls that Mapaputsi showed signs of having trouble adjusting to fame. He would occasionally disappear, but this time not into his music but into alcohol binges. 'I've been around artists my whole life and I always see the signs. As soon as they start drinking more before shows and not being able to handle gigs, that's when the alarm bells start to go off.'

Mapaputsi says he didn't plan on becoming a cautionary tale about the ills of fame. Life just happened that way. 'I try not to focus on the negative and the past, but I have to acknowledge that there were mistakes that I made. One of the things I allowed was for people who didn't have my best interests at heart to use me as soon as I started to make a name for myself.'

By the time Mapaputsi had to record *Kleva* a year later, he was spiraling downward, and it didn't help that his best friend Khabzela was incredibly ill. 'Khabzela was like a brother to me. We would have a lot of conversations about family, about dealing with success. He helped me more than he needed to because he was just a kind soul. It was really hard seeing him fall ill like that and knowing I couldn't help him.'

D-rex remembers the recording sessions for *Kleva* being the hardest of his life because Mapaputsi was so out of it. 'He would just lay in studio and we had to record and re-record things and I would piece them together because it was just not working. I don't know how we finished that album,' he says. 'If you listen closely to *Kleva* there's a lot of instrumental build up and repetition, which isn't really Mapaputsi's style. It's because I just had to create something to fill up the spaces.'

Despite all these difficulties D-rex and Mapaputsi somehow managed to finish recording the 11-track album. *Kleva*, surprisingly, is Mapaputsi at his most buoyant. Like the artist himself, the record is self-aware, wit-infused and deceptively funny. It is a kwaito masterpiece anchored by rhythmic perfection and a vivid rendering of the transition from obscurity to fame, and the afflictions that come with money and power. 'I was very unsettled emotionally at the time and I think you can hear a little bit of the intensity on the record. It's definitely more reflective than *Izinja*.'

One of Mapaputsi's greatest gifts as an artist is one of the hardest to quantify. In *Kleva* he showed just how superior he was to everyone else at picking beats and catching pockets of flows. Mapaputsi is most praised for his gravel-like voice, which is in itself his finest instrument, but the lower registers are where you find the real man. He is often referred to, rightfully, as an MC, but he tells me he isn't as interested in titles and labels now as he was when he was younger. 'I don't like to be defined by a single genre because I draw inspiration from different sources. Yes I make kwaito, but that is not my only home. I need to explore other sounds and influences without feeling like I am confined.'

What many might not know is that *Kleva* was a diss track directed at Ja Rule. The New York MC, who at the time was deep in the throes of his beef with 50 Cent, visited South Africa in 2003 and dissed South African musicians, saying they sang nonsense. Mapaputsi took exception and addressed that in the song. 'Who is he to say that and question us about our sound and music? So I was saying he is speaking nonsense he mustn't look down on us, we come from Jozi where real things happen,' says Mapaputsi.

Kleva was a hit and it's ominous instrumentation captured the zeitgeist of the moment. It was immortalised in an SABC advert where a young white man switches roles and experiences what it's like to navigate South Africa the way young black men do. 'I love that advert because it showed us what a lot of people went and still go through. Everywhere you turn as a black man, your presence raises suspicion and people look at you sideways.'

In war, they call them 'alive day memories'; the day where something catastrophic happens and you almost die. For Mapaputsi that was the day Khabzela departed and joined the choir in the sky. 'It wrecked me,' he says. 'It just...,' he pauses as if travelling back in time to the that day. 'It just wrecked me.'

Mapaputsi left Ghetto Ruff and began recording *Last Man Standing*. Easily Mapaputsi's most half-baked album, the record features three remixes from his previous records and an outro. Only six new tracks appear on the record. *Last Man Standing* opens with *Woza Friday*, one of the last kwaito tracks by him I really connected to. I remember being at home on 16 December 2004 and hearing it on Ukhozi FM, blasting from the speakers put outside in the yard of one of my neighbours. I stood at the traffic circle which was at the peak of a hill and looked down at the rest of the township. I will never forget that view. The air was thick with the smell of something; the possibilities seemed infinite. But now I know that smell was the end of innocence.

'There was a little bit of pressure to follow up *Kleva* because it had been so successful, and we didn't really have time to craft *Last Man Standing* fully,' he recalls. This was the beginning of the end of Mapaputsi's wave at the top of South Africa's music food-chain. What makes me admire Mapaputsi is that he embraces himself; he remains authentically himself even, at times, to his own detriment. His elocution of his approach to his craft has allowed us to peel back the layers of a life lived constantly on the edge. It's this that has allowed him to shine even through his most mediocre career intervals. He is not run down, even though 'iLife isikorokoro'.

There is an unforgettable video of Mapaputsi, wearing a grey jersey and a red shirt that sticks out from below and through the collar. He is wearing a big-faced watch and looks a little high or a little drunk or a combination of both. He is rapping to a trap beat about haters, money and women. All three things which I imagine he once had and still desperately craves but which now taunt him; unattainable, elusive. It's a heartbreaking video. A reminder that a musician dies twice. The second time is when the spirit leaves the body, which is the death we can all expect as inevitable. The first death however is when the muse leaves. This first one is way more cunning because, despite the evidence of history, no musician thinks it will happen to them. But it will happen; it always does. For Mapaputsi, the muse left in the summer of 2007 and hasn't been back since.

Change is pain

That year he released *Still Barking*, a record that sounds more like unpolished B-sides than an actual album. It confirmed what I already knew but didn't want to admit; the conclusion of an age of gods. The end of a love supreme. The thrill was gone.

It would be easy to ridicule Mapaputsi today, viewing hilarious, heartbreakingly desperate videos of him rapping. But there was a time when he epitomised the kwaito avant-garde. Nowhere is this more apparent than in his music videos, many of which often had a surreal sci-fi edge to them. And these visions of black dystopia are part of Mapaputsi's extended universe and artistic legacy. Think of the men in suits and ties whose lips ballooned whenever they gossiped in *Manga Manga Business*, or the levitating, gravity-defying shack in *Kleva*. These images all come together to intersect and create an interesting representation of an artist punching above his weight in terms of attaching metaphors to his work. Talking about one of these stunning video productions, Mapaputsi explains:

> We had a team from Tank Films in Belgium make the video for *Kleva*, and it cost R750 000 because we had to rig eight cameras and build a shack inside a plane. I didn't eat for three days because I needed to be light, so when we flew above the fly zone we could actually do what we wanted and I could actually flow.

When kwaito's voice fell silent, all protocols for what it meant to be a musician changed and in many ways the artists, the industry and the fans are still battling to piece together the scattered shards. As a means of self-preservation Mapaputsi has been forced to swallow the bitterness. During his nine years in the wilderness, he admits to suffering severe bouts of depression and feeling like the friends he thought he'd made in the industry had turned their backs on him. He also confesses to being turned off by the fiercely competitive musicians with nightmarishly jealous streaks, who he saw rise to the top of South African music. 'When we were making music it was all about unity and working together because we wanted to feed our families. I've seen a lot of youngsters who want to succeed so badly that they trample on other people, but they're still embraced by the industry. I want no part of that game,' he says.

Mapaputsi is defiant even in the face of the multifold defeats that come with being an artist trying to make his way out of his nadir. He has remained, for better or for worse, a fully-formed person. To exist so fully against the backdrop of such persistent ugliness has been his biggest victory. 'Nobody can say Mapaputsi did this or that to me. I am proud of the fact that I can go anywhere with my head held high and be respected because of that.'

Part of the reason why Mapaputsi was driven to oblivion was not his lack of creativity or inability to innovate, it was that he was trying to operate in a new environment using old tools. Mapaputsi is first and foremost an album artist. Sure, he has singles and hits but to get a fuller sense of his arsenal and a more in-depth picture of the man and his demons, you have to move past the confines of the singles and dive deep into the albums. It's here that he blooms most beautifully.

At the height of his career piracy began to take root in South Africa. People would copy his CD's using power DVD and Nero and bootleg them for R30, which then seemed like a bargain. Now you can get an mp3 genre mix of your choice with a few hundred songs for a mere R10. Mapaputsi is one of the artists who didn't try early enough to move into singles and craft a brand that allowed him to tour extensively. He had an incredible catalogue and a visceral need to express, but he lacked the outlet. 'The industry changed fast and that is why now, with the music I'm making I am thinking more about singles and not rushing to craft an album. It's sad because I really enjoy making albums, but they are hardly worth it now.'

With recent singles like *Inja Embi* he has been trying to call back the muse in an ever-uncertain music climate. These days he surrounds himself with younger artists; mostly DJs and rappers who help him record and back him up at performances. To them he is a god, to him they are a new lease on life. Integrity is not a word you hear often in music, but Mapaputsi has it. He tells me he always triess to teach younger artists that kindness is cool. 'They teach me a lot about social media and getting the music out there, and I try and share information with them about crafting songs. It's always refreshing to share ideas.'

Mapaputsi is a dancer in the dark trying to step back into the light. Retention of artistic autonomy during a period of reinvention is not something you often see in music, but he is working hard on that. Let's talk for a moment about reinvention. At the Red Bull Beat Battle held in Sun City about midway through his Top Boyz set, AKA brings out Jub-Jub. Eight years after he, at the peak of his career and high on drugs, ploughed into and killed four children, he had clawed his way back to the mainstage.

Jub-Jub's case had included a lengthy trial in which friends and family of the four dead schoolkids had to hear in excruciating detail the moments before their loved ones' deaths. But that all seemed a distant memory when Jub-Jub did a media tour upon his release and even released a song with Tshepo Tshola declaring just how much he'd changed and how sorry he was. As he stood on the stage holding hands with AKA and his Top Boyz posse at the Red Bull event, Jub-Jub seemed like even he could hardly believe it. His transformation was complete. And as everyone around him, including the fans, sang his *Ndikhokhele* all he could do was mostly smile. Relief.

Now let me tell you how this moment was won. After he was released, Jub-Jub released a track called *Shooting Star*, a mid-tempo hip hop number with an RnB hook that seems stuck in the nineties. But the song's lyrical content is what matters. Using the track's feel-good, anthemic vibe, Jub-Jub made it a point to praise and shout out every South African rapper that matters and say what he loved about them. Thus, in one sweeping stroke, he removed the target on his back. How can you beef with the gospel rapper who went to jail and came out not bitter but praising you?

A year before Jub-Jub was released Mapaputsi had released a remix of *Shooting Star*, but it wasn't as effective. The track was Mapaputsi praising himself, and it certainly didn't get him booked for any sold-out moments of redemption. Instead he toils at gigs in remote venues like Bekersdaal. 'It's a tough business but I appreciate the love I get from people. People still know the songs and sing along and that is what keeps me going,' he says.

The image is a hard one for me to adjust to. I still think of Mapaputsi as a superstar even though he doesn't have the cars, the gold chains or any of the costly accessories to suggest he was ever even one. In an age where we constantly harass ourselves with images of celebrities and their money, access and excess are what the public gaze hungers for and feeds on.

Soweto, because of its roots, is a township that has never known how to be silent. As a result it is a place that has given birth to a lot of joyful noise and streetsmart men and women who seem to know all the angles. Mapaputsi in this way is not unique; in fact he is part of that lineage.

He has lived in Soweto all his life. I call Mapaputsi from a café in Durban north that is playing an acoustic cover of 2 Chainz's *Freebase*, sung by a youthful-sounding white woman with a laboured, whispering, raspy voice. Over the phone, Mapaputsi confesses that it's not easy anymore. Soweto is killing him, he jokingly tells me. 'I should come live in Durban hey, the weather is nicer and it's quieter.' Places tend to respond to the impulses of their inhabitants, I tell him. He just laughs.

We are idealistic about kwaito but the fact is that it ruined a lot of lives. Mapaputsi is just glad to have survived. He's telling me how he almost clinched a TV deal for a reality show documenting his comeback, but it fell through at the last minute. 'That's just the way it goes," he says. I chuckle before I put the phone down. I want to dial back and say it also goes the other way round too, but I don't. This turns out to be the last time we speak, and the conversation is one of the best I've ever had. Talking to Mapaputsi you become increasingly aware of how well he has adjusted to life out of the spotlight. On an emotional level at least. Mapaputsi isn't going to be the superstar that he once was and that's okay. He is already something even more important: happy.

IV

Plagued by hypermasculinity
Esinako Ndabeni

MODEL C BY BROTHERS OF PEACE does not sound quite as funny and progressive when listened to with hindsight, considering that Ignatius 'Dr Mageu' Ntshebele died a convicted rapist in prison. Ironically, the last project he was working on before he died was his album for a rape accused Zuma, *Zuma for President*.

Mageu's gravelly voice and carefree, risqué style resonated with me because of the way he challenged respectability politics. He was a man of the street, a kasi boy who did not attempt to be anything other than what he was, in both speech and persona. I would hear older people expressing disgust or shame at how crass his language was, but I strongly believe in disrupting the way that order has been constructed in society. Also, the things he said were kind of funny. I had built him up in my head to epitomise the antithesis of classed notions of propriety and pretence. His digs at Model C students were funny to me as a Model C, and I read them as poking fun at our snobbishness.

However, on learning about the fact that this man had died a convicted rapist, the import of the song changed significantly for me. It was only after this that I began to note how the song made no reference to boys who had also been educated in Model C schools; it only poked fun at the girls. A song that I previously liked for its disdain for the classism that results when some achieve upward social mobility in black communities, started sounding more like a song about the frustrated contempt that men develop towards women they don't have easy access to. Of course, this is the best case scenario because the worst case scenario is that Mageu was actually singing about girls *still in* Model C schools, which would be even more predatory.

Mageu sings about how these girls demand things that he 'can't afford', such as pizza and hanging out in Midrand, Sandton, 'lokhu nalokhu nalokhu' (this that and the other). Of course, shaming women for their preferences or choices is not something that is exclusive to kwaito music. It happens across different strata of society. When a woman is not easily accessible to a man it seems to always become a problem.

Even as we are taught that men are providers, there's a simultaneous backlash against women who expect men to be the providers that they claim to be. On *Model C* Mageu goes to town lyrically about how impossible Model C girls are with their many demands. The real problem becomes clearer as he eventually gives up, saying, 'angeke ngiyimele mina lento, ang'namali futhi mina' (I won't stand for these demands, besides I have no money). Here he is finally stating the real problem: the reason he will not stand for the 'nit-picking' of Model Cs is that he doesn't have enough money. Writing this in a cultural moment where transactional relationships are a hot topic, I've come to understand that money is a big part of how masculinity is constructed. I too have been proposed to by men who assumed that their wealth would be enough for me to pay attention to them.

When young women engage in transactional relationships with older, wealthier men, it becomes difficult for men who are either younger or not as wealthy to have access to these young women. This creates a violent aggravation that comes with ridiculing and slut-shaming these young women because, while the patriarchy has determined that women's bodies are for the consumption of cis-heterosexual men, women should not be able to choose which men may consume their bodies in ways that disqualify other men.

Mageu's aggression when dealing with Model C girls becomes clearer and clearer. At one point in *Model C* he proudly proclaims that when these girls ask him to introduce them to Oscar (now Oskido), he asks them what's in it for him. When these girls decline these sly advances, Mageu does not shy away from disclosing that he dismisses them or won't let them meet Oskido. The lyrics are quite frankly alarming, showing how it is issues of male entitlement that drive this disdain for Model C girls. One is left concerned by the kind of lyrical content we enable in the name of artistic expression and a groovy beat and how this affects the actions of those who consume and produce such content.

In a country like South Africa where where rape culture has become so normalised and rape is a national emergency, it almost feels like a losing battle to insist that we hold artists accountable for the kind of language they use. My time revisiting kwaito music and researching the culture has become increasingly disillusioning. Every other day there is new information that a kwaito artist has been implicated in sexual assault or domestic violence. One by one, all the people that I have built up as heroes in my head fall away like dominoes. It was reported in 2017 that South Africa has the highest rate of rape in the world. This ought to make rape an urgent crisis that has us all panicking and committing to rectifying behaviour that enables rape culture to survive in South Africa.

Since there is a link between language and action, there is a link between the way kwaito's men, and by extension black men, sing about women and how they will treat them. Music, especially genres as rugged as kwaito and hip hop, is given leeway to express alarming ideas about women. And yet, incredibly, when it comes out that an artist has sexually assaulted a woman or a child, there is a shocked public outcry even though the warning signs are often in the lyrics we ignore.

Vulgar language

As far as morality and language goes, I'm naturally inclined to having quite an affectionate relationship with vulgarity, viewing it as protesting imposed ideas of propriety that often have very little to do with how we affect other people on a systematic level. Our response to language, like our response to the gender-based crimes that artists commit, is plagued by sensationalism. By and large, I don't believe that, for all the gender-based violent crimes that men in kwaito have committed, their relationship with vulgar language ought to be one of the things we see as a sign of violent proclivities.

What is more alarming for me than artists using swear words is the response to the 'nakedness' of female kwaito acts such as Boom Shaka's Lebo Mathosa and Thembi Seete. That is where our ideas about rape are created. Women were commonly portrayed in music videos as half-naked video girls for a long time, but it suddenly became a problem when young women artists chose to image themselves in that same way and make money off it. It's ironic that we exist in a society that encourages entitled ideas about how women and girls choose to dress themselves and yet there is (a performed) outcry each time a man beats up or sexually assaults a woman. This is the real monster in the room: that men have been allowed to determine the narrative of womanhood.

So I'm not particularly interested in thinking through the vulgarity of kwaito with its use of swear words, because our ideas about propriety are also rooted in insidiously classist and sexist ideas of conduct. The very construction of the prototypical 'gentleman' as chivalrous and well-mannered concerns me. Not only is it a classist and racialised idea but it has also created a more covert kind of entitlement in men. And this is coupled with an internalisation of that entitlement in women.

This is clear even in 'gentlemen's' engagement with rape. I've heard many gentlemen make the supposedly reassuring assertion that sex with a willing partner is more pleasurable than sex with a person who is not willing. The problem with this is that there is no such thing as 'sex with a person who is not willing'. That is rape. More importantly, the fundamental problem with this narrative is that it centres the pleasure of these 'gentlemen' in a conversation about rape. Our conversations about what constitutes 'good' men are plagued by this very same thinking which undermines the struggle to dismantle rape culture and, by extension, patriarchy.

The idea persists that if a man conducts himself with a certain level of debonair civility, a kind of performed kindness, then he ought to have an easier time convincing a woman to be with him sexually. It makes women trophies who are mute rewards to men for their decency. It becomes a formula: if a man is 'good' or 'nice', then he should get women as a reward. What we see when these 'good men' or 'nice guys' do not get the girl is a disgruntled 'nice guys finish last sulk-fest, which is often followed by violence when the man eventually stops bothering to be 'nice'.

Subsequently, our conversations about rape culture need to dig deeper into the normal, everyday conduct of men as opposed to indulging in this window-dressed concern. We should identify red flags and act on them accordingly, instead of criminalising rape and not patriarchy in its entirety.

The response of 'proper society' to kwaito artists was that they were deemed amavuilpop because of their chosen style of dress and love for Iscamtho or Tsotitaal', a language that many people still associate with criminality. The fact that kwaito's men swaggered around in a way that did not hide that they were kwaito artists and men raised in the township, was also weaponised to prove the level to which they were not proper 'gentlemen'. The unspoken assumption is that because these men are amavuilpop, it should then surprise no one that they would be implicated in rape claims. That, in fact, they should be expected to be capable of such violence. I want to question this idea of policing black expression under the guise of dismantling hypermasculinity, because the black state is always assumed to be aggressive. As Frantz Fanon has said, black people are imagined to be emotional where white people are rational. Proceeding from these deeply entrenched stereotypes it is easy to dismiss kwaito music as a passionate performance of hypermasculinity. However, I would argue that there is space for black men to express themselves without falling into the pit of toxic performances of masculinity.

State and media hypocrisy

Limited and limiting approaches to dealing with gender-based violence are visible even in the way that our government deals with issues. For example, the 16 Days of Activism campaign against gender-based violence has come under fire from feminists both young and old as we have thought through what it means to dedicate only 16 days to rigorous activism against something that happens every day. Last year, in 2017, the Institute of Gender created a hashtag #EverydayPerpetrators. Under that hashtag, people expressed the importance of being active daily and rigorously against gender-based violence.

One of the conversations that came up was the irony of the ruling party rallying behind 16 Days of Activism when the Zuma rape trial was still fresh in our collective memory. When Fezeka Khuzwayo, known at the time as Khwezi, accused the then former deputy president, Jacob Zuma, of rape, women clad in ANC Women's League regalia saw it fit to carry around placards with words such as 'burn this bitch'. These words were directed towards a young woman who was coming before the courts to say that she had been violated in a way that is extremely common in South Africa.

South Africa went on to elect the very same man as state president. And yet, whenever it's that time of year and 16 Days of Activism comes around, the same political party that responded to Khwezi in such a vile and dismissive manner takes to the podiums and airwaves to express 'real alarm at the rates of gender based violent crimes in South Africa'. Quite frankly, the jokes write themselves. We are a country of people who are complicit in perpetuating rape culture but become shocked when rape happens.

The way in which incidents and allegations of rape by kwaito artists have been reported in the past by our media seemed to be geared more towards sensationalism than genuine concern and a desire to dismantle rape culture. *DRUM Magazine* titles would exclaim in big, bold letters, 'ARTIST'S RAPE SCANDAL: EXCLUSIVE'. This was rape being treated as nothing more than 'the big scoop', and magazines took great pride in covering such stories first as 'exclusive' news items. But rape is not a scandal. It is a systematic issue that needs to be dealt with every day.

There is not a day in my life where a man who is a stranger to me does not harass me on the street while I dither about whether I should just smile and ignore him or tell him to fuck off and end up a statistic of young girls raped and killed by men. Every single day. Somehow, the urgency of this crisis does not permeate through our engagements with popular culture, and we are often uncritical of potentially violent ideas being passed down through music.

In 2017, singer Busisiwe 'Cici' Twala, who was signed under Arthur Mafokate's 999 record label and was also his girlfriend at the time, posted a picture of herself with her broken pelvic bone and the hashtag #BreakTheSilence. The message behind this was clear; Mafokate had abused her. It is difficult to police the actions of two consenting adults, so I don't know how much of a case I can make for intervention in Mafokate's dating patterns. However, it seems that for a long time Mafokate has had a habit of dating young female artists that he signs on to his 999 record label.

True to form, our media has always reported these relationships as 'exclusives' – scoops that were more important for breaking the story – with very little work being done to raise alarm at the fact that Mafokate has a longstanding habit of dating his very young protégés. Power is not something that men do not use to assert their dominance over the women they date. It is always there in the relationship, looming large.

When someone like Arthur Mafokate chooses to be in a series of relationships where he wields total power, with what are practically his young employees, it should raise alarm about the kind of ethics that this man has. There should have been more interrogation of this disturbing pattern and the consequences it had the potential to have. What happened to Cici and whether it was a repeat occurrence remains unclear, as there has been little interest from the media to investigate this story. When Cici posted that picture on Instagram, Arthur Mafokate merely locked his Twitter account so that people who didn't follow him couldn't see his posts. He only unlocked the account when it seemed that people had forgotten about the incident.

Needless to say, he unlocked it in no time, because we forget gender-based violence very quickly and easily in South Africa. The same magazines that had reported Mafokate's latest artist girlfriend as hot news were the same magazines that wrote about how shocking it was that Mafokate had abused his girlfriend. The very same magazines that had never thought to track Mafokate's dating habits and raise an alarm about his dating patterns, were now writing about the allegations that Mafokate had abused his girlfriend as though it was something unthinkable. Again, the jokes write themselves.

In the case of Brickz, there seems to have been a public consensus that his act was despicable and he belongs in prison. It was not that difficult to see how vile Brickz was to perform this act; the victim was his 16-year-old niece. Wasn't that the narrative on the news? 'Brickz found guilty of raping 16-year-old niece'. It is no secret that discourse around gender-based violence in South Africa relies on 'out-of-the-ordinary' episodes. Often, to appeal to men who don't seem to understand the gravity of the crisis, we say, 'Imagine if it had been your sister, your mother or your niece.' Now, when it comes out that a man raped his *niece*, the moral conscience of many rises in contempt of this perverse act. You can't slut-shame a 16-year-old niece.

How differently public sympathy would have played out if it had been a 21-year-old woman, perhaps even a fan of his. I suspect that speculation about the motivations and veracity of the rape allegation would have ensued. In a country where the vulnerability of black women has been proven many times, I still get the sense that black women have to be vulnerable in special or extraordinary ways before they are deemed deserving of society's empathy.

A question that we all need to ask ourselves, all of us, whether we're into kwaito or not is: do we want our black voices to be voices that erase or violate the experiences of black women? It is disillusioning and a shame that we are now left with the burden of thinking through how we engage with these men as pioneers, people who were active in a hugely significant moment of making black South African youth culture, but also as women abusers and rapists who are increasingly being outed for their violent and abusive ways.

Gender-based violence and abuse is a systematically enabled epidemic. As I have highlighted in this chapter, gender-based violence is not a sensation that only warrants reaction when it has become monumental enough to make headlines. It is in the things we laugh at, the words we say, the songs we dance to. We have a responsibility to root it out even when it seems harmless. Because a joke about how demanding girls from Model C schools are in a country where men have used violence against women's bodies as a last ditch attempt to regain seemingly lost power, is not all that funny if you think about it.

V

Arthur Mafokate: Kwaito's most hideous man?

Sihle Mthembu

In a moment I will tell you why Arthur Mafokate is often wrongfully credited as the king of kwaito and doesn't really deserve that title. Not simply because he is not the genre's foremost innovator (that title could go to a Mdu or a Spikiri), but because he represents a toxic masculinity and a co-opting of the very notion of artistic autonomy, placing him at odds with the aspirations of black excellence and joy that are at the core of the music's roots. But first let me tell you about the exact moment I fell in love with kwaito and how I got to the place where I had that momentous experience.

In the summer of 1998 my mother and I took an hour-long drive to a remote village in the KZN midlands called KwaHlathikhulu. The village had three schools, each one designated to a different area, which at the time was under the control of the Inkatha Freedom Party (IFP). This latter fact meant that the village was still blackballed from accessing basic services such as running water and sanitation, with the ruling ANC government tying political loyalties to the provision of basic services.

The village community had to walk 5 km to fetch water in communal taps, and for the first time in my life I experienced what it was like to use a long-drop toilet, also known as a pit latrine. At the time it felt like I had travelled back into the Stone Age. In the small township of Bruntville where I was born and raised, we had more civilised amenities, like the bucket system. Thinking back on this irony now, I can't help but cringe. 'Consciousness takes time,' the writer Thando Mgqolozana once told me.

On the day of our arrival we met the paternal side of my mother's family. It was the first time we were coming face to face with them after my mother had spent years trying to find them. My maternal grandmother, Freida Vilakazi, after experiencing a bad breakup with my grandfather, had taken my mother and returned to her family vowing to never again speak his name, an oath she kept for a quarter of a century. One day my mother asked where she was from and my grandmother refused to say. My mother persisted, asking again and again until grandma eventually told her about this village, KwaHlathikhulu; a place surrounded by trees and red earth. Our children always make us break our promises.

KwaHlathikhulu was also the first time I had seen people with so much land. The home had a large garden, three separate buildings which had two to three rooms, and a stand-alone kitchen. There was a kraal full of cows and a yard that was easily 20 times the size of the yard I'd grown up in, which was saying a lot because we had one of the bigger yards in the township of Bruntville. They had a garden which was teeming with spinach and maize. Every day my cousins would come back from school and fetch the cows which were grazing on the nearby hills and after that saw wood to make the night's fire. This was the first exposure to a more nuanced idea of what it means to work; to the idea that labour and liberation were connected.

But when I first visited it wasn't the black mold on the inside roof of the kitchen hut or the graves of my relatives in the middle of the yard – monuments to a forgotten past that grabbed my attention. Instead I noticed the TV. See, back home in Bruntville we had a small 37 cm TV set. It was black and white and grainy and often it would have to be moved between the kitchen and the living room so we could get a better signal. But here in a remote village, my mom's family had a full colour TV screen. It was almost twice as big as the one we had at home and sat regally in a room divider in the lounge.

The day we came to visit for the first time was the last day of school, but my mother had insisted on taking me with because I'd already received my report confirming that I was going to the third grade. I think she also took me because she wanted me to experience this place with her, unsure if there would ever be a second visit.

When we arrived only my great grandmother was around; an ancient woman with no teeth in her mouth and cheeks that had collapsed in on themselves. Her skin was so wrinkled it was soft to the touch. She dished up isijingi, a yellow pumpkin porridge, and I was so disgusted by it I pretended to be sick. My mother suggested I should go and sit in the lounge while they sat in the kitchen next to the warm fire. This was strange to me because where I come from we only made fires in the evenings, but here they kept it burning all day. Later I would learn that my grandmother cooked the pumpkin porridge in the afternoon so that when the children came back from school they wouldn't starve.

Back then I was convinced that my acting sick had worked, but I know now my mom and great grandmother had more important matters to talk about. Like ending 25 years of silence. How do you thaw a cold car? How do you get it to start up again so it can take you where you need to go? So there I was, a boy left in the living room to watch TV on his own. I can still hear the sound that those brown fake-leather couches with wooden armrests made when you sat or even moved on them. I took a seat just behind the blue and white door, directly in front of the TV and away from the light.

Given free reign of the remote for the first time in my life, I struggled a bit to find the channels. Did I mention that our little 37 cm black and white screen back home didn't have a remote? This was during the time when SABC would turn to Channel O or CNN during the day. Luckily for me it was Channel O that day, and, after several false starts, I got to see some of the best videos of the year in living colour. This included Mafokate's *Oyi Oyi*, a stomping township ballad in which a possessive boyfriend questions whether his woman has a new man in her life. 'May'vuv' uyajola? So'yabona bona?' (Baby you got another man? You're acting smart now?), he asks, singing with an infectious nonchalance.

In the video, Lebo Mathosa plays Mafokate's elusive, alluring love interest. She is a township femme fatale, wearing a purple dress that doesn't completely conceal her underwear, hair tied up in her signature high-tied frizz. She never responds to her cuckolded lover but shimmies throughout the video as Mafokate confronts her with questions. About a minute into the video comes the moment I was telling you about earlier; the moment I feel in love with kwaito. Mathosa walks away from Mafokate, who is wearing all black and brandishing a gas canister, presumably to set shit off. Mathosa opens the door and jumps into the front seat of the convertible car and he thinks she is going to sit down. Instead, she floats across the front seat and gets out on the other side, leaving him blue in the face. I wouldn't be surprised if this moment was unscripted.

I had seen things like that before in movies; delectable, seductive women whose power was in how unattainable they ultimately were. But never a black woman. Never in the same music space that I occupied. Never like this. Mathosa does not even smile in the video, rubbing in how she is toying with him. She intends to be and remains elusive. I imagine I must have let out a slight squeal when I saw that. In the years which followed, whenever I watched that video this is the moment I would always pay close attention to, making my way back to it time and time again.

We need to talk about Arthur

The stories we tell ourselves are often merely a vehicle for justifying how we got here.

Arthur Mafokate stood in the dock of a courtroom, wearing a designer black jacket and jeans. For most of the time his hands were in his pockets, as if he was resisting the urge to fiddle.

He had a look of casual indifference, as if the court proceedings were a minor inconvenience and he'd much rather be getting on with his day. Mafokate was facing charges of assault after his former artist and girlfriend, Cici, pressed charges against him. According to the pop songstress, she and Mafokate had been involved in an altercation that turned violent, and the kwaito legend beat her severely and dragged her in the street with his car. Mafokate in turned filed a counter suit in which he alleged that Cici had been the aggressor and had hit him with a hanger. Nobody was buying it.

Occasionally Mafokate whispered to his lawyer and eventually the case was postponed for a third time, after Cici and her team refused a motion for mediation between the two parties. It's difficult to imagine that Mafokate was once one of South African music's kingmakers. He attained the title of 'king of kwaito' by keeping a distance between his label and other artists, over the years dividing the genre he had helped create. Today this had come back to haunt him. Mafokate looked around the courtroom and he was alone.

Cici, on the other hand, was supported by fellow musicians and victims of abuse, as well as civil rights groups. TV presenter Andile Gaelesiwe, herself a survivor of abuse who in 1997 had participated in a *Next* magazine shoot with Mafokate where the two embraced and smiled ear to ear, was there to support Cici.

Things fall apart, they might take time but they always fall apart.

Poet and musician Ntsiki Mazwai, who has long been a critic of Mafokate and his 'grooming' of his female artists, was also among the court attendees. She was vocal outside court. 'Why are you surprised by Arthur when he has had power and control over all his women artists? These men must stop being too comfortable with violence. Arthur has been exploiting young women in the industry for years.' Mazwai would later state on Twitter that she had been raped by Brickz while they were in a relationship.

It's incredible that even in this era, where identity politics set the agenda and intersectionality is at the center of every conversation we hold dear, Mafokate still has a place in our culture. He somehow seems to have fast-forwarded past the #MeToo moment simply because of the clout he has built for himself over the course of his career as a kwaito musician. Despite charges of serious abuse pending against him, none of his supporters seem to have distanced themselves from the musician/record label owner. He is still snapping selfies with national government leaders, visiting radio stations and gracing magazine covers to 'tell his side of the story'. The video for his gqom-inspired single *Welele Le,* which was released days after a court appearance, climbed up to a million views on YouTube in less than three weeks, proving to the naysayers and the newcomers what many of us have long known: Arthur Mafokate is scandal proof.

But before all this, the early signals of a man kicking into gear a well-formulated crisis plan started to show. In the weeks following being charged, news surfaced of how Mafokate is seeking counselling after the assault on Cici, and how he is using the incident as a moment to reflect. He also started posting more and more pictures of him and his children on his Instagram account, cultivating the image of loving family man and doting dad.

When researching Mafokate, one trope becomes glaringly clear. He is adept at the art of playing victim as far as the female artists-cum-lovers in his life are concerned. There is a startling headline from a 2004 copy of *DRUM* in which Mafokate is referred to as the 'King of broken hearts'. In the article he speaks about the end of his long, very public relationship with Abashante frontwoman

Queen Sesoko. Mafokate blamed the singer for the end of their relationship and said he had felt 'abandoned' by the singer.

Even further before that in 1998, Mafokate did an interview in which the headline read, 'The heartache of the kwaito king'. In it he detailed the emotional toll of having been single for a year following his break up with Tsholo, one of the backup dancers of Abashante. Tsholo would later be released from the group under unclear circumstances.

There is a scene in the 1944 film *Gaslight*, based on the play by Patrick Hamilton, in which Gregory (played by a buoyant Charles Boyer), a man who has been manipulating his wife into thinking she is going mad, is tied up to a chair by the wife, Paula (played by Ingrid Bergman). She finally confronts him about all that has sent their marriage off the rails. Her movement is calculated and deliberate. 'There've been times when I thought I only dreamt those days,' she says. Self-victimisation and alternative presentations of reality are the key tools in the arsenal of hideous men, and Arthur Mafokate is no different.

To understand how Mafokate got to be this way you have to look back. Not just to the time when he released hit songs like *Kwasa Kwasa* and *Mnike* and got a second life after pundits had written him off. You have to look back further than *Oyi Oyi* and *Kaffir* to a time before he positioned himself as the most talked about solo act of his day. You have to look back at where he came from.

Sello Arthur Mafokate was born in Dobsonville in Soweto in 1984. This is the same year that the ANC upped its campaign of civil disobedience in the area. The son of famous horse rider Enos Mafokate, Mafokate is one of five children, including his brother and fellow kwaito star Oupa aka Makhendlas. Growing up, Mafokate and his family were poor but he notes that the importance of art was always emphasized in his family, even from an early age. 'My parents loved listening to music and they always tried to tell me about the bands that they were into. It left a very strong impression on me to always be in a house that was brought alive by music.'

Mafokate and his nuclear family unit were divided when his mother, Grace, left Dobsonville for rural Lebowakgomo, where she worked as a nurse at Groothoek Hospital, taking the kids with her. Enos stayed in Johannesburg to continue living his dream as a champion show jumper, and was absent during some of Mafokate's most formative years. 'It's difficult to have your dad and not have him. You start to question whether you were the reason why they weren't staying in the same house even though they were still together. It was also hard just for my mother to raise kids and work and have to worry about whether we were okay,' he says.

As early as 1985 Mafokate recorded his first demo at Spokes H's Black Talent studios. The track, titled *Working For A Living*, was however never released and the demo was lost. According to Mafokate, to fill the void created by the absence of his father he took an interest in soccer, dance and music, inspired by the exploits of pop megastars like Brenda Fassie and Sello 'Chiccho' Twala. Through his dance group, he would later work as a backup dancer for Fassie, Monwa & Son and Johnny Mokhali.

He used this experience to refine his moves and understand what appealed to mass audiences. These dance routines would also become a defining and essential accompaniment to his music. With moves like *kwasa kwasa, qopetsa, sika lekhekhe, mnike* and *hlokoloza*, Mafokate ensured that he not only set the agenda for what people listened to, but how they moved to it as well. 'Movement is an instinctive African thing. It's like you are empowering your body when you move. For me I don't understand how you can separate dance from music,' he says.

Mafokate's attraction to fame and the spotlight also led him to dabble in other things. In 1992, having returned home to Soweto, he won the title of Mr Soweto. By this time, Mafokate had developed a fierce competitive streak after years of entering music and dance competitions. As part of a trio called Out Of Control, he had won the Kool Aid Dance To Stardom competition in 1989. The trio also won the Soweto Dance competition for three years in a row from 1989–1991. 'What those competitions teach you is how to put your best foot forward because you didn't have time to mess around. You mess around, you're eliminated. So everything you do has to be decisive and spot on,' he says.

As collaborators fell by the wayside, Mafokate would find in Joe Nina an equally committed musical peer. The duo, under the name Q-face, entered the Coca-Cola Full Blast Music Show where they sang *I Need It*. The song became a fan favourite and gained the youngsters some notoriety, putting the industry on high alert. Mafokate participated in two subsequent seasons of the music show, using the time to showcase his range as producer by dabbling in gospel, Afro-pop and early incarnations of the sound we now know to be kwaito. Having been rejected by labels in the past, Mafokate used the prize money from competitions to buy his own equipment and build his own studio. This studio would become known as 999 Records, so named as a tribute to the little house in Soweto where he'd grown up.

Producer Tronix Madibe who was a long-time collaborator of Mafokate's before they split due to financial disagreements, recalls those early days in the studio. 'Arthur always had a plan to be the biggest star South African music had ever seen, even when he was starting out he was very ambitious and driven to do anything to succeed.'

Having started as an engineer, and through working with the likes of Taboo and the New Age Kids in the mid-nineties, Mafokate reinvented himself as a one-man hit factory. Despite his music being one-dimensional he became a working-class hero because of the relatability of his story. Here was the archetypal young boy from the township who had risen by any means necessary and made it to the top.

He was also fiercely independent. Who can forget the splash he made when he released *Kaffir* barely months into our democracy and snatched the wigs of every conservative South African still peddling notions of rainbow-nationhood. The controversy also gave Mafokate a template for generating publicity by being kwaito's provocateur-in-chief.

'The thing is South African audiences can be very conservative. It's always good to give them something to talk about,' he says. 'But art is also about being ahead and making a statement about how things are changing. When *Mnike* and *Sika Lekhekhe* came out they were controversial. Now you have people twerking on social networks and nobody bats an eyelid. It's all about the timing,' says Mafokate. 'What most people don't realise is that radio stations banned *Kaffir* but the people made the song what it is and loved it, and it still did well. So people were always going to be against kwaito because the masses were driving kwaito and nobody could control that.'

He followed *Kaffir* by simulating anal sex on stage at the SAMAs in protest of the award ceremony's judging categories and rules and one thing became very clear: the guy was a star and we couldn't keep our eyes off him. 'You have to always be pushing the envelope especially when you are at your prime. A lot of artists always feel like they will do things and say things when they are older. We made it clear that we would not be kept in chains and made to play by unfair rules.'

Mafokate's music is at best uninventive and formulaic; hard beats full of drums and percussion are looped and repeated, and phrases in which he adlibs in between the hooks and bridges are inserted. This is then capped off by a final verse, often delivered by a female vocalist. In *Haibo*, 'haai bo' is the repeated phrase and in between Mafokate shouts out his friends and artists, and Queen does the guest verse. She also does the same on *Oyi Oyi*, where the title is the repeated phrase and in between Mafokate asks questions. On *Mnike*, 'mnike' is the repeated phrase and so on and so forth. His songs are a collection of leitmotifs parading his peculiar brand of instructional masculinity. The songs are full of passive-aggressive jubilee.

Mafokate is great at simulating being a good artist; his genius is not necessarily that of the creator but that of the problem-solver. He is a persistent tweaker of formulas until he hits the right public note. He works with others in the building stage and then goes off on his own when it comes to refinement. It's here that he does his best work. Choosing vocalists, choreographing dances and setting up schemes to market his work are his strengths, and his recipe worked for years, until it didn't.

The defining trauma of Mafokate's life was not in receiving death threats for making *Kaffir,* or spending years away from home and his father. Instead it was something that happened after he had reached superstardom. It was the death by suicide of his younger brother Oupa 'Makhendlas' Mafokate.

Tragedy strikes

By all accounts it was a beautiful send off, whatever that means. Among the attendees at the memorial service were star soccerites Thabang Lebese and Fani Madida, who at the time were the bread and butter of Kaizer Chiefs, the club Oupa supported, unlike his brother who to this day remains a steadfast Orlando Pirates fan. The likes of Tshepo Mabona, Thembi Seete, Mfundi Vundla and DJ Fresh were also in attendance. During the two-hour ceremony, Radio Lesedi DJ Thuso Motaung invited artists to come on stage and give one of their own a musical send-off. Vuyo Mokoena, Zwai Bala and Rebecca Malope's voices filled the hall with a rendition of *I Know The Lord.* Mafokate did not join them on stage; all he could do was sob in the front row.

Three days later, on a chilly Saturday morning, Makhendlas's body, dressed in a black and green suit, was brought into Gallagher Estate Hall where mourners were allowed to pay their last respects as the tragic idol lay stiff in a bronze-and-gold-plated casket. What everyone agreed on was that it shouldn't have come to this.

Makhendlas had been booked for a concert in Mpumalanga along with 999 Record Label mates Abashante, Chafkop, Stitch and New School. Before the show, Mafokate had an uneasy feeling because the venue was changed at the last minute from Nelspruit to Naas Stadium in Tonga. He had been attacked there once and wasn't sure his brother going there was the best move. But by then it was too late; Makhendlas was one of the headliners and could not be cancelled. 'I knew something was wrong and looking back I feel like I should have trusted my instincts,' says Mafokate.

Just as Abashante were about to go on stage three shots rang out and the stadium descended into chaos. Then there was a fourth and final shot. 'It was like time stopped. Everyone didn't know where the shots were coming from, we didn't even get to perform and then we heard what had just happened. It was surreal. Oupa had just been with us and now we were being told he was dead,' recalls Nestum.

Makhendlas had gotten into an argument with a fan that was taunting him. By all accounts nobody knew Makhendlas was carrying a gun, or that he even owned one. During the altercation he shot 18-year-old Thulani Vilane in the toe, right leg and then the stomach before running to a nearby parking lot and shooting himself. Vilane, who was then a Grade 9 pupil in Nelspruit, survived the shooting. Makhendlas didn't.

Makhendlas was an accidental superstar; one of Mafokate's own making. He had initially planned on being an architect. One day when he was washing dishes, Mafokate called him into the studio and suggested he record a song with him. Oupa agreed, recorded and thought nothing of it. Weeks later en route to town, he recognized a song on the radio as the song he and Mafokate had made. The track sold over 50 000 units and the legend of Makhendlas was born.

For years Mafokate blamed himself for his little brother's death and feared the public did too. If only he hadn't introduced his brother to music. If only he had gone with him that day. If only he had been there to calm tempers. If only. If only. When we talk about Oupa, Mafokate's voice fades as if regret is engulfing the sound and he can no longer form the words to make the world bearable again. 'I would lay awake at night. All I knew is that if I was there he wouldn't have done that. He would have thought twice.'

Oupa, who was a devout Catholic and regularly attended church in Midrand not too far from where Mafokate lived and made music, was just 27 when he died. Despite the death of his brother, Mafokate reached his peak in the period between 1995 and 1999.

Record label boss/predator

Over these years he and his 999 artists, particularly Abashante, dominated the local music scene with their grooves and elaborate performances. According to Nestum, who had been introduced to Mafokate by Bongo Maffin's Speedy, Abashante was founded by Mafokate as a direct reaction to the success of Boom Shaka.

'We were all friendly but there was also a lot of competition. We wanted to stake our claim and say hey, you're not just going to run the show,' says Nestum. Through songs such as *Intwenjani* and *Settling The Score*, Abashante transcended kwaito and became a mainstream pop project with rap and bubblegum undercurrents. Through the group Mafokate wanted to create an aspirational image for young women, while using revealing clothing and suggestive dance moves to attract the attention of men. As Nestum points out, that attention wasn't always welcome. 'To his credit Arthur always warned us. He told us not to eat or drink things people gave us. He was always very cautious and sometimes it felt like a lot but it was solid advice.'

But apart from Abashante, it wasn't music that became Mafokate's primary project. Instead, it was his relationship with Queen Sesoko.

The two had an on-and-off-again relationship for the better half of a decade and over this period Sesoko, who refused to be interviewed for this book, had a child by Mafokate, Owami. The couple made headlines when Sesoko apparently left Mafokate and disappeared for days with another man. It was a national scandal. As Nestum puts it, the rollercoaster nature of their relationship affected Abashante's output and is what eventually led to the demise of the group. 'We were a family and obviously when one member of the family is not fine the whole family is not fine,' she says.

Mafokate has worked with women throughout his career and has tapped into the myth of female singers as muse. But on closer assessment, it's clear that things have never ended well for any of the women signed to his 999 stable. Sesoko was dropped from the label and went from music star to broke and living with her parents. Nestum left after no longer wanting to perform half-naked following her marriage to a Muslim husband. Purity was 16 at the time she signed for the label and complained publicly several times about her records being pushed back. Before Lira became Lira she toiled for years on 999, at times being reduced to a background vocalist. Mafokate eventually agreed to release her from her contract.

In her autobiography Lira details how she wrote songs that Mafokate would give to other artists, without even asking her for permission or informing her at the very least. One case in point is that of *You Can't*, one of the standout tracks on Queen Sesoko's debut album. 'I wrote a song called *You Can't Love Me* and had Queen (Sesoko) listen to it – and she loved it. While I was at home over the weekend, she recorded the song, describing it as her own. This broke my heart. She named it *You Can't*. The song was included as part of her album and I was hurt by the fact that no one bothered to ask me if this was okay. This was the first bitter pill I swallowed, and it made me realise that I had to look out for myself,' says Lira.

Despite having released an award-winning album with the label, Lira left 999 after just two years, citing 'creative differences'. She has since told News24 that her tumultous time there helped her develop her own model for navigating the industry. 'I am very grateful for the experience I gained at 999 Music. I had to learn from the challenges. I faced them. That was my university. I spent two years at 999 Music and learnt everything I needed to know about the music industry. I built a business model from what I learned.'

On the cover of her only album, Purity sits looking directly into the camera with her feet on the table, showing off her orange All Stars. The title of the album, *I'm Bad*, is embossed on the bottom right corner. Something about it calls to mind Aaliyah's debut, *Age Ain't Nothing But A Number*. A closer inspection of the cover reveals a hideous man was lurking in the background there too, both figuratively and literally.

Despite his countless transgressions, Mafokate continues to thrive as one of the central figures in the history of South African music and is arguably the most active kwaito legacy act. He has received endorsements from Smoothies for their Hall of Fame campaign and was even commissioned by the SABC to write a jingle as a relaunch of Dub, the cartoon character on SABC 2. He also regularly fills slots along with Chomee at ANC rallies. It is not uncommon to find him bouncing and gyrating on stage wearing green, yellow and black alongside the party's top six.

Mafokate has been hailed as an entrepreneur for his moves in the industry, but the truth is he is the opposite of black excellence. At his height he worked to ensure that only he and those close to him benefitted from the house he built. He has over the course of his career made himself a regular fixture in the psyche of the South African public, and his lowbrow aesthetic occupies an important place in the country's music heritage. But he is also a hideous man who has been allowed to get away with too much for too long. How, you ask? The answer is simple. We let him.

VI

Kwaito women
Esinako Ndabeni

IF COLLECTING INFORMATION ON kwaito is a mean feat, what do you call collecting information on women in kwaito? Because, boy...

'Amapantsula' has become a synonym for kwaito artists since male kwaito artists fashioned themselves after the pantsula culture, and because the genre of kwaito is dominated by them. The image of the 'kwaito artist as pantsula' has come to be taken as given, without interrogation, but it makes the main narrative of kwaito gendered – because the pantsula subculture is a masculine culture.

I still get the sense that the women of kwaito, some of whom, like Lebo Mathosa and Thembi Seete, were phenomenal forces on the frontlines in pioneering the kwaito revolution, are almost an afterthought in our conversations about the genre. Personally, my interest in revisiting kwaito as a young adult was born out of my rekindled relationship with the late, great Brenda Fassie. I had found myself listening intently to her kwaito album *Imali*, and it led to me reading more about her and revisiting old documentaries.

I remember watching Chris Austin's doccie, *I Am Not A Bad*

Girl, at a friend's house. I must have been 14. In the documentary, MaBrrr (as Brenda Fassie was popularly known) talks about her love for sex and vulgarity. She unapologetically discusses her 'devil-may-care' attitude, and I remember thinking that she cussed too much for my liking. It was appalling to watch. After all, I was being raised in a world where my aunts barely got to leave the house because they had to kneel on the floor and polish the stoep, and do the washing, and cook, and bathe the younger children and stay at home. In a world where, to resist this gender-typecasting, to be anything other than what it prescribed, was to be branded a 'nondatshaza' (street woman).

I was being raised in a world where my uncles could come home at whatever early hours of the morning they wished, because they were men. I was being raised in a world where I would be accused of messing around with boys if I came home late, long before the thought of being involved with a boy had even crossed my mind. In that world, girls and women had different, stricter criteria for respectability, and Brenda Fassie refused to meet them.

Five or six years later, having grown and learned about the rights that black women (like all women) have to self-determination, this same documentary filled me with a profound appreciation for MaBrrr. She was a queer black woman living her truth even when it was upsetting to other people. She had an awareness of what was expected of her as a black woman, and she still chose to defy all of society's prescribed notions of propriety. Seeing her do something as simple (but controversial) as sitting on the boot of her car with her legs wide open, was the kind of deviance I now understood and appreciated.

Up to that point, the sexually deviant black women in pop culture who had inspired my feminism were women such as Eartha Kitt and Nicki Minaj; women in American popular culture. So, for me to see this kind of rebellion against conforming, reflected boldly in the life of a black South African woman, was the dawning of a more relatable politic. My curiosity then led me to the discovery of other great kwaito female acts such as Boom Shaka, Mshoza and Abashante. Later on I decided that I wanted to write about these young female artists who had been able to assert themselves in such a male-dominated space. And so my love for kwaito grew again, from my childhood days of doing the 'guqangamadolo' to Mzekezeke's dance anthem.

Today I write about these women at a momentous point in time where feminism has made its way back into mainstream discourse and popular culture. And I write about these women as feminist icons. Of course, one should should be careful of stripping these women of their complex agency (by referring to them as feminists) when they have never made any claims to feminism. But a feminist icon, at least to me, is somebody who inspires my feminism regardless of whether they identify as feminist or not.

Women who managed to assert themselves, reclaiming their autonomy within popular culture, are my leaders. For me they are my feminist icons, especially because they risked and were met with considerable backlash.

Kwaito women and agency

Boom Shaka, with two young men and two young women, is curiously remembered mostly as a girl group. with much of the focus on the group being directed towards its female members, Thembi Seete and Lebo Mathosa. But Junior Sokhela and Theo Nhlengethwa were an integral part of Boom Shaka. While Mathosa and Seete were phenomenal performers, one cannot help but wonder how much their sexualised imaging (young women doing the latest gyrations in their crop-tops) had to do with this perception – this fixation that the music industry and music lovers continue to have with the consumption of women's bodies.

Male kwaito artists not only sang the words 'shake is'bunu

sakho, umzimba wakho' (shake your bum and your body) to and about women, they also invoked sexually objectified images of women in their music videos. Young women were constantly clad in bikinis and gyrating (as seen in TKZee Family's music video for the festive season anthem, *Fiasco*). True to the patriarchal notion that, 'men are providers', women are flaunted by artists who have acquired wealth to prove that they now have access to conventionally beautiful women, sexually and otherwise – even in this 'progressive' era.

Maud Blose, in her paper *Pornographic Objectification of Women Through Kwaito Lyrics*, argues that:

> … women's representation is most often in their value as back-up to the male artists, as sexual objects in male lyrics which have been known to be offensive and even violent, or in women's performances where sexuality and bodies are the agency which expresses their power as women on stage. Women aren't seen as the talent behind the music, but are seen more as 'highlighters', adding colour to the song through the explicit pornographic representation of their bodies.

First, I must highlight that I am wary of the use of the word 'pornographic' to describe the bodies of young black women who wear revealing clothes. Because of the gaze that coloniality has viewed the bodies of black girls with, it seems that it is too easy for the imaging of a black girl to be labelled as pornographic. There is an assumed perversion attached to our bodies, as Professor Pumla Dineo Gqola writes in the chapter, 'What's Race Got to Do with Rape?', in her book, *RAPE: A South African Nightmare*. Professor Gqola considers the stereotypes that racism tends to attach to black women – that is, the perception of black women's bodies as hypersexual. And truly, following on the legacy of the treatment of female African figures such as Sarah Baartman, our bodies are hypersexualised even before we have been able to think about what sexuality is. In my humble opinion, the idea that there were ever 'pornographic' representations of these young women's bodies continues in the same vein. Therefore, it is important that we constantly examine our reaction to the nudity of black women's bodies and understand how certain strong reactions trigger and are triggered by characterisations memorialised in history.

Now, Blose's assertion interests me because Boom Shaka diverged from the narrative of young, sexualised women as 'highlighters' in live performance or music videos, while still celebrating their sexuality. What makes the sexualised image of Thembi Seete and Lebo Mathosa so powerful, beyond the curiosity of its politics, is the fact that they were at the centre of the Boom Shaka kwaito juggernaut. They were not the decorations in the videos and performances, they *were* the videos and performances. As opposed to them being in the background to humour or adorn male artists, these artists were half-naked, winding and twisting their hips, in their *own* music videos. Lebo Mathosa built a name and brand so phenomenal that she was able to venture into acting, with a role on *Generations* and a cameo on *Backstage*.

Musically, Lebo displayed incredible versatility as she moved across genres, even making a power-move as an RnB singer in collaboration with legendary US RnB singer/producer Keith Sweat, on the song *I'll Trade (A Million Bucks)*. Lebo went as far as garnering comparisons to the incomparable Brenda Fassie, with some asserting that she was the natural successor to South Africa's most-loved, most talented pop idol and was similar to her in many ways. But Lebo, true to the unique camaraderie that these female artists with star quality seemed to have, never shied away from saying that she had no intention of living under MaBrrr's light, even though she had great affection for Fassie and felt honoured by the comparisons. And that was the enduring narrative – there were all these different women who occupied the same space differently, and they showed love to each other in their diversity. 'She was my favourite singer of all time,' Mathosa would tell Amanda Ngudle of

DRUM Magazine, in 2004, when Brenda's name came up.

It seems to me that Lebo Mathosa's talents were overshadowed by her hypersexualisation, both by the public and the media. Of course, having a noticeable sexuality and using it is a talent to pursue one's goals in showbiz, is not something peculiar to female artists. However, going back to Buyile Mdladla's 2001 profile of Mathosa in *Drum*, I could not help but be filled with regret. 'Lebo has been sculpted into perfection by Mother Nature, to be used as a torture device for men. Her sexiness oozes with her every stride, and every pout of her lips,' Mdladla writes. 'If you ever want a heart attack, just catch Lebo on the beach in a thong bikini,' he continues, and goes on to write about her long legs, her full lips, her 'skimpy, see-through outfit that doesn't leave much to the imagination.' On the role that Mathosa played on *Generations*, Mdladla writes that: 'Even that heavy role, jam-packed with sad emotion and thick with melancholy, contains a very sexual tone'.

It seemed that even in the moments where Mathosa was owning herself and building her legacy, men still imagined that she existed merely for their consumption. But this was later contradicted by the very same journo who'd painted her as 'a torture device for men'. Mdladla, in a more nuanced, more mature article, acknowledged that Mathosa did not fashion herself for the erotic fantasies of men. 'What gives me a thrill is when girls my age come up to me to tell me how much they appreciate my sense of style, or when high-profile celebrities like Zandi Nhlapo compliment me on my outfits', Mdladla would quote Mathosa saying in another article for *DRUM*. And she continued to live life on her own terms up until her tragic death at 29 in that car crash in 2006 that sent a nation's youth into mourning. I was nine years old then – it was all noise to me. But Lebo Mathosa left behind a legacy so monumental that, twelve years later, when I was finally able to understand what she signified, I was able to go back and try to make sense of what her legacy meant.

Thembi Seete, Louise to Lebo's Thelma, survived Mathosa's death. And she has survived the way in which kwaito has fizzled out, with many and varied career progressions. She did continue her career in music after Boom Shaka, most notably with the 2009 album *Music Is My Life,* featuring collaborations with music heavyweights such as DJ Cleo, DJ Tira and Big Nuz, and a Black Coffee remix of the album's opening kwaito spiritual, *Nkosi.* Beyond the music, however, Thembi would solidify herself as an actress in the post-kwaito moment. With roles in movies such as *Hijack Stories* and *Fools,* Seete cemented her reinvention as an actress of note. She has been a constant feature on prime time television, coming into her own as Hazel in *Yizo Yizo,* as Lerato in *Gazlam* and as Penny Moloi in *Zone 14.* A talented dancer and a fierce presenter, she enchanted the South African youth on *Jika Majika,* a TV show where talented dancers would come together and compete for cash prizes. To this day, Thembi is one of very few of the pioneering kwaito generation who have stood the test of time. She has also had roles on the e.tv soapie, *Rhythm City,* and recently landed a radio gig on *The Afternoon Drive* at Massiv Metro, which she co-hosts with Zola 7. From those days of 'provocative' clothing and dancing, the women of Boom Shaka clearly made names for themselves (and money) out of something that has so often symbolised how women are disenfranchised in society.

Back then, it looked like Boom Shaka had come up with a winning formula – a group that centred female artists and had a raga artist giving the masculine edge. Abashante, formed by Arthur Mafokate's 999 record label, certainly seemed to replicate the Boom Shaka formula. Queen 'Iyaya' Sesoko and Zanele 'Nestum' Nyakale were the central focus of the group, with Abel 'Aba' Golepe (later replaced by Tebogo 'Zombo' Ndlovu) providing the rugged raga element.

I am aware that the imposition of my feminism onto this narrative may not be completely accurate, as I try to make sense of the actual lives of these women. I recall an interview that Nestum had with *DRUM,* for instance. In that interview, Nestum proudly claimed that Mafokate had 'tamed' her, as she had been a bit of a tomboy who cussed occasionally before Mafokate 'disciplined' her. It is curious and unsettling for me to read that someone like Nestum had to be 'disciplined' into becoming this smiling girl in crop-tops and tight pants, gyrating in music videos. Even the name 'Nestum', like that of another of Mafokate's protégés, the late Purity, has a disturbing perversion to it. Who would name a young woman, growing into herself, after a soft food for babies?

While Dr Angela Impey misinterprets kwaito as an apolitical genre in her paper, *Resurrecting the Flesh?: Reflections on Women in Kwaito,* she is accurate in her observation that kwaito, 'appropriated defiance as a fashion statement'. And that was exactly the point about the women of kwaito: they *defied* the ideas of what a respectable young woman was meant to look like. They *defied* the notion that girls could portray sexualised images of themselves only if it was for the consumption and benefit of the male gaze, and never out of sheer enjoyment or for the possibility of making profits. And they made it a fashion statement.

Of course, I find myself going back and forth with these ideas, as I do have to consider the difficulties and contradictions that women face in navigating patriarchy. Maud Blome writes quite perceptively about this in her paper. Blome contends that, while it is possible to understand the ways in which young women took advantage of the commodification of their bodies (by making their own profits off it), it is also important to understand this as something taking place against the backdrop of the commodification and exploitation of women's bodies in a broader sense. Therefore, while women can exploit patriarchy in order to survive and even to profit within its prevailing conditions, this is still done against the backdrop of patriarchy.

Even a figure as iconic as Brenda Fassie, for all her defiance, has raised many questions about the treatment of female artists in the music industry at that time. Even posthumously, evidence of this has come to the fore. When her only child, Bongani Fassie, announced that a biopic would be made about Mabrrr, Chicco Twala boldly proclaimed that it would not happen without his approval because he has all the rights to Brenda Fassie's music.

Ntombizodwa Makhoba of the *City Press* newspaper reported that Twala's lawyers had written a letter stating that, 'In terms of the said agreements, Twala was granted commercial exploitation rights on the feature film of Brenda Fassie. Twala respectively holds 90% of Fassie records and [has an] 82% shareholding in Estate Late Brenda Fassie, with Bongani Fassie and Estate Late Brenda Fassie holding 10% and 18%, respectively.' Bongani later disputed these claims, stating that he has all the rights to his mother's estate. Whatever the case may be, it is incredible to imagine that Twala ever owned that much of Brenda Fassie's work. And it certainly does a lot to complicate the framing of Brenda Fassie as a 'Madonna of the South African townships'– a powerful woman in control of her own business and destiny.

In her piece titled *Brenda Fassie: The Gender Context*, for *The Con* magazine, Gwen Ansell writes about how a young male colleague of hers in Botswana was once sent to interview Brenda. The young man arrived for the interview, only to be told that a man from her management would answer his questions himself, while Brenda was instructed to 'look after' the young journalist. What the 'looking after' entailed is left up for speculation, as it was merely implied and not explicitly stated.

But it is frightening to imagine the possibility that this rebellious icon of a woman might have been pimped out by her management at some point in her career. Even Desmond Mulatana, who was part of The Big Dudes, would say, as narrated by Gwen Ansell, that they (The Big Dudes), had 'managed to control her and she listened when [they] called her to order'. A figure I regard as my feminist icon had men who instructed her to 'look after' young male journalists, and men who felt that they could 'control' and 'call her to order'? It certainly suggests that the story is a bit more complex than just a reclaiming of agency by women who refused to conform to the expectations of patriarchy. And it raises many questions about the treatment of female artists in the industry.

To avoid writing about kwaito in a way that continues the understanding of it as a boy's club is a dream that any feminist writing about kwaito should have. However, the problem with attaching collective identities onto individual bodies is that these bodies can refuse to participate in the collective narrative-making. Simply put: one cannot go banging on somebody's door to force them to tell their story, for what they imagine to be the bigger picture.

There seems to be a hesitance on the part of many of the big female names in kwaito to speak about their experiences. The 'why' can only be left up to speculation. It's a complex undertaking, representing women who have not expressed the desire to be represented. But I must write about them, because writing about them is writing about myself. It is an investment into how I can understand myself, how young black women like me can understand themselves and how other people can understand us.

Mshoza and Thandiswa Mazwai: A divergent aesthetic

A defining moment for young women in kwaito was Mshoza's entry onto the scene. From the moment she got voted into first place by Loyiso Bala on *Jam Alley* in 1999, Mshoza would come to solidify herself as a formidable female lyricist in kwaito music – able to hold her own in songs with kwaito lyricists as talented as Mzambiya, who was also signed to BullDawgz Entertainment. And all this while she was still a teenager.

Mshoza had already made her first million at fifteen. Her song *Kortes*, from her album *BullDawgz' First Lady*, is still a largely referenced kwaito classic today. I, too, fondly recall being a small child in my rural home, with my terribly unkempt, relaxed hair that desperately needed treatment, doing the choreography to *Kortes* as seen from the music video. With her deliberately 'deep' voice and street mannerisms, Mshoza showed that girls are not a one-dimensional stereotype, as she deviated from the female kwaito artist's image that had previously dominated the scene.

Her stage name gave notice of this intention to rewrite the rules, to be fair. A 'mshoza' was supposed to be the female equivalent of a pantsula, although the term would later be diluted to mean the women who chose relationships with pantsulas. Mshoza refused to fit neatly into the existing narrative of female kwaito artists (as far as imaging herself in revealing clothing) because her persona did not centre on how she looked or danced. Instead, she spat bars on a beat and made a hit song. She still remains the only female kwaito artist to be clothed by Loxion Kulca.

Wandi Nzimande, the co-founder of Loxion Kulca, recounts for me in a conversation we had about women in kwaito, that Mshoza was often referred to as a 'tomboy'. This was a deliberate, perhaps even surprising image for her to have chosen, considering that she had previously taken part in local beauty pageants. Despite this departure in how she presented and comported herself as an artist, to the young women in kwaito who had come before her, Mshoza still chose to celebrate them as aspirational figures. The young Mshoza hailed Lebo Mathosa and Brenda Fassie on her song *Mshoza Yi Bhoza*, singing, 'Bang'biz' uSuperwoman njengo Brenda Fassie noLebo Mathosa' (They call me Superwoman, just like Brenda Fassie and Lebo Mathosa).

Thandiswa Mazwai, as part of the group Bongo Maffin (and in kwaito at large), also carved out her own niche. First, the Bongo Maffin sound was deeply-rooted in traditional Xhosa music and afro pop – quite different from the dance music that other kwaito artists were making. Mazwai was keenly aware of the uniqueness of the Bongo Maffin sound. This much is clear in the *After Robot* documentary, where a young Mazwai passionately states, 'If you listen to house and you listen to the drum pattern as a black person, you can move to it. I think it's because white people move to the tweeters and we move to the bass.' Shortly after this, she breaks into a Xhosa folk song. Despite her entry as a prototypical kwaito artist in the group Jacknife, Mazwai soon developed a distinct kind of interest in the music, which stood out from the approach that other female artists in kwaito had. Her aesthetic was that of the young Afropolitan woman – long skirts with traditional prints, Converse All Star sneakers and the occasional Xhosa-style face paint on her face. But she was still bold enough to remove her wig and get her hair shaven in a music video, as we saw on Bongo Maffin's *Thath' Isgubhu*.

Mazwai was resolute that her participation in kwaito would see her unapologetically laying claim to her own choices in music-making. Too often, writing about women in kwaito has to centre around ideas of sexuality. But Mazwai was strictly about the music – and that is what she has stayed true to all these years. After 2005, she went on to become the only member from the then disbanded Bongo Maffin to dominate on the South African music scene. This started auspiciously with her iconic debut solo album, *Zabalaza*, in 2006. This album communicated Mazwai's politics – as a black woman who had an investment in her history as a young, Xhosa, South African. At the same time, she gave an emphatic nod to her kwaito roots in that album's typical kwaito, bass-thumping track, *Kwanele*.

And she has lived her life the same way since, both as an artist and as a woman. Since going solo, Mazwai has built a formidable brand for herself – a solo career so monumental that I broke into tears when I missed her performance of her jazz album, *Belede*, at the Cape Town International Jazz Festival in 2017. Because 'King Tha' (as she now calls herself, having evolved from her previous moniker, 'Red'), is bold enough to venture into whatever genre of music she desires to venture into. She has championed the voices of women; even women who are not deemed to be 'respectable'. Lebo Mathosa, who fashioned herself very differently from Mazwai, is one of the women whose legacy has been protected by Mazwai herself. In a conversation we had on Twitter, Mazwai would tell me that people once thought they could use her image to denigrate Lebo, who had fashioned herself in a more risqué manner. But Mazwai was having none of it. And she has fought hard to stay true to her politics.

As a show of solidarity, she even hosted a women-only bash on 31 March 2017 in honour of her birthday, and repeated it the following year. Her iconic women-only birthday bashes now seem set to become an annual fixture on the local music programme and feminist agenda. The parties have an all-women line-up of artists and only women can attend, creating a safe space for them in a world that constantly threatens and erases them. While I risk sounding like I imagine all experiences of womanhood to be dichotomised and compartmentalised, I want to argue that when women who are different from each other show support to each other, it makes space for every kind of woman to exist and to succeed.

A shoutout to Zodwa Wabantu

There have been many black women in popular South African culture who have received public backlash for their deviance. Today, the same thing can be seen with Zodwa Wabantu's rise to fame. Popular for her dance moves and the Savanna bottle she always holds in her hand, Zodwa Rebecca Libram has become a household name, with a great deal of her fame attributed to her sexual appeal. Since making it, Zodwa has also revealed that she previously engaged in transactional sexual relationships with men in the past, in order to make ends meet. There has been a great deal of controversy around the kind of clothing choices made by Zodwa and the ease with which she admits to her 'sexually deviant' behaviour.

Performing at a festive season show in 2017, Zodwa explained to her fans how she uses her body to her own benefit. Clad in a two-piece bikini, Zodwa said, 'So, ladies, we have power. Use your power. Uyabona nami ngisebenzis' indunu yami, uR35 000' (Look at me, I'm charging 35k for people to watch me shake my ass). At the end of her controversial motivational speech, she said, 'So nani zifebe zami, sebenzisani indunu yenu' (So you all, my bitches, you should also use that ass to make a profit). Be yourselves. Don't change. Don't give a fuck).

Bitches. Hoes. As much as it is derived from the derogatory word 'whore' and was made popular by misogynistic men in hip hop, 'hoe' has been reclaimed by young women to represent the freedom that women should have to own their sexuality. In a bid to be unashamed about our sexuality and sexual choices, young women have chosen to explore their sexuality under the Twitter slogan, 'hoe is life'. This is because the survival of slut-shaming depends on the shame that women who have been labelled as sluts feel when it happens.

For Zodwa to explicitly tell people that she is using her body to get ahead, it means that she has no shame about it. Therefore, it is a politics of reclamation. You cannot shame someone who is unashamed. This moment brings into sharp focus our continuation of the kwaito women's legacy, especially the Brenda Fassie and Lebo Mathosa legacy – the imaging of the black woman who, to put it in my own words, simply does not give a fuck. Naturally, people found Zodwa Wabantu's statement inflammatory and there was backlash. A few female celebrities even joined in to criticise Zodwa for her actions.

DJ Tira, Zodwa's manager, later announced to social media that he needed to have a meeting with Zodwa about her strong language. Following this, in an Instagram video made for the public, DJ Tira gave an indication that Zodwa would be changing her language and asked Zodwa to tell the fans herself that she would change. Zodwa then states that she will change her language, neatly sidestepping the idea that she will change herself. And Zodwa has definitely not changed her language since then.

I don't have to make the case for representations. But the representation of young black women in kwaito as contested figures who took up a space that did not accommodate them, is a representation that has filled my generation with hope. As feminists become increasingly controversial, as they let go of older, more respectable forms of feminism, a better understanding of women from the past also arises. It is important to think of women in kwaito as figures who defied the barriers placed on black feminine bodies, while also understanding them as young women who were participating in a male-dominated industry, with mostly men as management. This latter point may complicate my ability to position these young women as totally autonomous figures, but they were certainly torchbearers in an ongoing striving towards autonomy. These women remain iconic, and the significance of their contributions is understated.

Brenda Fassie. Lebo Mathosa. Thembi Seete. Nomasonto 'Mshoza' Maswanganyi. Zanele 'Nestum' Nyakale. Queen 'Iyaya' Sesoko. Sharon Dee. Thandiswa Mazwai.

They made dance anthems. Movements. They disrupted patriarchy. They paved the way.

VII

On kombuistaals and tsotsitaals
Esinako Ndabeni

TODAY, TSOTSITAAL IS A LANGUAGE best spoken by the older population. The figures who popularised the language on television, such as Dominic Tyawa who played the role of Bra Gibb on *Yizo Yizo*, and Darlington Carmichael (the infamous Georgie 'Papa G' Zamdela on *Isidingo*) remain as iconic references to the dialect, which does not seem to be passing down to the younger generation on a scale comparable to before. A linguistic code that began as the preferred language of the young, hip and urban in black communites of the sixties going forward, has lost its popularity amongst today's youth as Iscamtho becomes the new township lingo of choice.

The generational difference of these two urban black dialects is brought into sharp focus in the movie *Hard to Get* (2014). The movie features well-respected actors Jerry Mofokeng and Israel Makoe. These two thespians, both admired for their mastery of what we might call 'township dialect', showcase the fundamental difference between Iscamtho and Tsotsitaal. Makoe's character, while clearly speaking a tsotsitaal (lingo associated with the streetsmart and criminal in urban ghettoes), bases his language on isiZulu, while Jerry Mofokeng's is richly interspersed with Afrikaans. The conventional languages that Iscamtho and the original Tsotsitaal are based on are therefore different.

My interest in tsotsitaals began when I discovered that kwaito got its name from the 80s gang called Amakwaito, whose name derived from the Afrikaans word 'kwaai'. Except, its meaning deviated from the standard Afrikaans meaning. It seems that this word which means 'angry' in conventional Afrikaans, was understood to mean 'cool' in township lingo. Having spent quite some time in Cape Town, I realised that coloured people from there spoke a very different kind of Afrikaans from the kind we were being taught at school. They called it 'Kombuistaal'.

I thought I'd embark on a journey of trying to understand how it is that, in a country characterised by segregation, Kombuistaal had made its way into Tsotsitaal. I started off basing my research on the understanding that kwaito artists used Tsotsitaal as their main language of communication. However, this turned out to be untrue.

Kwaito, having emerged well after the Soweto-led uprisings, is a genre that mostly relies on the use of Iscamtho. Of course, in kwaito's early days some Tsotsitaal did feature in the music, beyond the realisation that there is some historical intersect between the two dialects and some words occur in both. Take one of the earlier songs for example: Arthur Mafokate's *Daai Ding*. As the chorus of the song goes, 'Daai ding is nie reg, man. Phansi ngodlame'(That thing is not right, man. Down with the violence). However, this use of the Afrikaans-heavy Tsotsitaal did not become a common feature in kwaito, which grew more disposed to Iscamtho, with its base of isiZulu and some seSotho. I choose to call these two urban dialects 'tsotsitaals' to stress first of all that they aren't one and the same thing, but secondly to emphasise the fact that both these lexicons are township lingo associated with criminality.

Today there is probably no doubt in black communities that the Afrikaans language was used to further entrench the oppressive agenda of the apartheid regime. However, as much as this has become the majority view amongst black people today, the entymology of Tsotsitaal is perhaps an indicator that this was not always the case.

There was a point in the history of black communities when people adopted Afrikaans and recontextualised/repurposed it, as evidenced by the heavy Afrikaans influence in original Tsotsitaal, which has its roots in the urban black townships of the 1950s and 1960s.

Professor Ana Deumert from the University of Cape Town (UCT) makes the case for understanding Tsotsitaal as 'a form of cultural-linguistic appropriation or even parody; taking the language of the oppressor and making it one's own', which clearly frames Tsotsitaal as an ingenious form of contestation against the imposition and hegemony of Afrikaans. Put in another way, it was an attempt to turn the language of the oppressor on its head and undercut the language imposition.

However, the fact that Afrikaans was such a major component of Tsotsitaal suggests that opposition to the language as a form of linguistic and cultural oppression was not quite as keen as became the case after the 1976 Soweto-led uprisings. In their article titled *The Structure of Tsotsitaal and Iscamtho: Code switching and in-group identity in South African townships,* sociolinguists, Sarah Slabbert and Carol Myers-Scotton, argue that the 1976 Soweto uprisings marked an attitude shift among black people against Afrikaans. The turning point came, they argue, when the apartheid government announced that Afrikaans would thenceforth be the medium of instruction in black schools, in furtherance of the Bantu Education Act of 1953.

As the record shows, this draconian measure was met with stiff resistance and would go on to become a pivotal moment in South Africa's history. It was because of this, Slabbert and Myers-Scotton argue (citing Albert Ngwenya), that the youth began to gravitate more towards the isiZulu-based Iscamtho and away from the Afrikaans-based Tsotsitaal. Afrikaans became an outright symbol of oppression (more than it already had been?) Perhaps the tongue-in-cheek adoption and subversion of Afrikaans made sense as a form of protest, until the apartheid regime attempted to institutionalise its use as a medium of instruction in black schools.

However, another version of the history of Afrikaans that has gone largely unexplored and understated is that which traces the roots of Afrikaans as a language that was founded by coloured slaves in the Cape Province. In this version of the sociolinguistic history of the language, Afrikaans was founded by slaves in the Cape, delegitimised (only to be appropriated by those who call themselves Afrikaners today), and later repackaged to black people as a white language of oppression. This narrative has not quite made its way into mainstream discourse. Perhaps this is because it is a complex and emotive topic to grapple with on both ends of the racial extreme.

The whitewashing of history typically enables white people to perpetuate narratives that best serve them, so there has been little engagement about the topic from academia, which remains largely white and eurocentric. Furthermore, if black people's engagement with Afrikaans as the 'oppressor's language' is anything to go by, then there has been little space for black people to probe this discussion objectively or meaningfully. Throughout South African universities in the last few years, we have seen a resurgence of militant activism against the rampant culture of white Afrikaans in universities such as Stellenbosch, the University of Pretoria and the University of Free State. In this, we see the weight of Afrikaans and how its use by the apartheid government has made it a difficult subject to engage with in a manner that takes all its nuances into account.

A brief history of Afrikaans

As Dr Neville Alexander narrates in the documentary titled *Afrikaaps*, leading up to the 1850s, Afrikaans was perceived as a kombuistaal (kitchen language), as it was the language of the 'servant class' in the Cape. Dr Achmat Davids (1990), who refers to the language as a 'creolised Dutch', echoes this idea as he says that this creolised Dutch was mostly spoken in rural districts of the Cape, while the upper class and 'more cultured' Christians resisted it.

Davids narrates the story of Afrikaans, tracing it from when the Dutch arrived in the Cape where the Khoi and San people were living. With their colonial logic, the Dutch decided that Dutch was the only language that was legitimate, and they would begin to impose it upon the Khoi and San people.

One can only imagine the kind of Dutch that the Khoi and San people were speaking, rich with their own linguistic influences. The importation of slaves from other parts of Africa and South-East Asia further infiltrated Dutch as spoken in the Cape, incorporating lexical influences from different languages such as Malay, possibly Portuguese (some of the black slaves had been brought in from Angola) and the Khoisan languages. This language, this creolised Dutch, came to be known as Cape Dutch.

It was not quite recognised as a legitimate language but was a bastardised Dutch that the brown people along with poor white farmers spoke. It was often referred to as a 'kombuistaal' or 'Hottentotstaal'. The Muslim community of the Cape, the Malay, were perceived as the best representatives of the language. Historian Saarah Jappie explains this best here:

> Malay speakers, as part of the city's underclass, were illiterate in the Roman script. However, because of their knowledge of the Qur'an they could read and write Arabic. Joining these two skills, they adopted the Jawi system, using Arabic letters to write Malay. By the early 19th century Malay was losing ground to Cape Dutch, an early form of Afrikaans. Quite soon, Cape Dutch became the lingua franca of the Muslim community, used as the official language of religious sermons and in the madrassah setting. In order to write the new language, the Jawi system was adapted and Arabic-Afrikaans was born (Jappie, 2015).

Cape Dutch was not well-received by the more affluent classes in the Cape and was often mocked and delegitimated. These notions of propriety in language, of course reflect themselves in Tsotsitaal as well. This is why the history of Afrikaans is important to highlight: respectability politics are at the core of the legitimation of language.

It is widely accepted that the word 'kaffir', which came to be a slur word denoting black people, came from the Arabic word 'Kafir', which translates to 'unbeliever'. How reflective is this of the poor Dutch farmer's misappropriation of Afrikaans, a creolised language that was spoken by Muslim people of the Cape? I'm imagining a situation where the Dutch settlers heard these Malay people talking about 'Kaffirs' and, sensing its negative connotations, decided it sounded so bad that it would be the perfect word to define black people...

In 1875 the Genootskap van Regte Afrikaners (GRA) was formed. The GRA (meaning 'the society of real Afrikaners') was formed in an attempt to standardise this Cape Dutch. Except that it was no longer called Cape Dutch, but christened 'Afrikaans', and it now belonged to white people. Today, they identify themselves as 'die regte Afrikaners' (the real Afrikaners) and until recently there has been little contestation around the legitimacy of that claim.

The language Afrikaans would grow to become a symbol of Afrikaner nationalism. This appropriation called for the purging of recognisably non-Dutch lexicons.

Dr Neville Alexander notes that 'dankie' is in the Afrikaans dictionary today but 'tramakassie' is not there as a synonym. The rich history that tells the story of the servants in the Cape would become erased and whitewashed. Eventually, Afrikaans become the language of apartheid. In essence, a language that was formed by diverse, intermingling, oppressed groups was appropriated by an oppressive group, to be remembered solely as a symbol of their oppression of other groups.

What does Kombuistaal have to do with Tsotsitaal?

Slabbert and Myers-Scotton use Gerhard Schuring and Dumisane Ntshangase's research, published respectively in 1983 and 1995, to trace Tsotsitaal back to the Amalaita and Funani gangs which were active in the area known at the time as the Witwatersrand (present day Gauteng) in the late nineteenth century and the early 1900s. I suppose this is reflective in the name of the language itself, for it translates literally to 'thug language'. Slabbert and Myers-Scotton assert that the base language, the language that is the common ground among Tsotsitaal speakers, is Afrikaans. None of the available scholarship seems to disagree.

The strong influence of Afrikaans is indeed quite evident when one hears Tsotsitaal. In its very name, it is referred to as a 'taal', the Afrikaans word for 'language'. However, what is more interesting to me is thinking about the *kind* of Afrikaans that Tsotsitaal seems to base itself on. While, as I explained earlier, Afrikaans was standardised and sanitised by the so-called 'Afrikaners', the older kind of Afrikaans: Cape Dutch, Kombuistaal, creolised Dutch, remained resilient in the Cape.

The general attitude I picked up during my high school and varsity years in Cape Town is that the Afrikaans spoken by the coloured community is accepted as a kombuistaal while 'standard' Afrikaans is called Suiwer Afrikaans. Spending a part of my high school years in a coloured area called Pelican Park, I picked up some Kombuistaal. Of course, I had no idea that there were all these politics behind the language and it was just a very cool version of Afrikaans in my mind. I recall writing an Afrikaans essay in Grade 9, narrating what had happened during the weekend. 'Dit was gevaarlik, my bru!' I'd concluded. My Afrikaans teacher, a white woman, was very confused about why a weekend spent playing games at the Canal Walk and attending church was so dangerous. Of course, I meant that my weekend was cool. Kombuistaal, no longer a 'bastardised Dutch', is now understood as a bastardised form of Afrikaans.

As explained earlier, the word 'kwaai' (the very word that kwaito derives itself from), means 'angry' in Suiwer Afrikaans. However, in Kombuistaal today, the word 'kwaai' means 'cool.' The 'kwaai' in the gang Amakwaito's name, and later, the music genre, was understood to mean 'cool' by township blacks. I will illustrate the differences in how the word would be used across Suiwer Afrikaans, Kombuistaal and Tsotsitaal, below:

Suiwer Afrikaans: 'Daardie man is kwaai'. (That man is angry.)

Kombuistaal: 'Daai man is kwaai'. (That man is cool.)

Tsotsitaal: 'Daai man is kwaai'. (That man is cool.)

Note how the Kombuistaal and Tsotsitaal sentences are completely the same. While the word 'daai' has made its way into the Suiwer Afrikaans understanding, it is not a standardised and respectable word. The word is more likely to be heard in the Afrikaans spoken by brown people of the Cape. It is for reasons such as this example that I'm interested in the kind of Afrikaans that Tsotsitaal uses as a base. Another example of this is the use of the word 'gevaarlik', also meaning 'cool' in Kombuistaal as well as Tsotsitaal. In Suiwer Afrikaans, 'gevaarlik' means 'dangerous'.

To this day, Afrikaans-speaking people in Cape Town incline towards code-switching; moving between Afrikaans, English and inserting the Arabic lexicons that have remained. This is also a common linguistic behaviour among Tsotsitaal speakers, for the language itself is a fusion of the many black languages that intermingled in the townships.

What makes the issue complex is South Africa's history of segregation. Logically it would make sense for Tsotsitaal to be based on Suiwer Afrikaans, because that was the language that proliferated and was imposed on black South Africans. In fact, Slabbert and Myers-Scotton write, borrowing from Janson's research, that newcomers to the city were more proficient in Afrikaans than English, as a result of having worked for white farmers in the Vaal. However, Tsotsitaal also bears witness to the interaction between coloured and black people in the townships. There seem to be two narratives that account for this linguistic exchange:

- **Some of the leaders of the numbers gangs were coloured men:** Slabbert and Myers-Scotton trace Tsotsitaal back to the Amalaita and Fulani gangs that operated in the Witwatersrand from the nineteenth century up to the early 1900s. These gangs would later break up to form the numbers gangs; the 27s, 28s and the Big Five gangs. Some of the leaders of the latter three gangs were coloured men. This interaction would significantly influence the kind of language used by 'tsotsi' (criminals).
- **Tsotsitaal having its roots in pre-forced removals in Sophiatown:** This narrative, as told by the sociolinguist Professor Ana Deumert, does not necessarily contradict the narrative above. Deumert writes about Sophiatown as a multilingual, multi-ethnic space before black people's homes were demolished and they were forced into townships such as Meadowlands. This is where Deumert has traced the origins of Tsotsitaal to. This space facilitated exchange and interaction across racial lines and could account for the presence of coloured people's lingo in Tsotsitaal. Of course, in this narrative the figure of the 'tsotsi' is also present as the figure who introduces this language into the township.

There seem to be differing accounts for the definitive historical moment where/when Tsotsitaal was formed and popularised. In the main one, two important schools of thought about the origins of the language emerge. The first is that Tsotsitaal was formed before the Group Areas Act of 1950 was introduced. If this is so then it would not be so far-fetched to contend that Tsotsitaal was based on Kombuistaal more than it was on Suiwer Afrikaans. Of course, because of the dominance of the so-called Afrikaner, there are limits to this argument, because the effects of an imposed language are more far-reaching than those of a language born out of contact and collaboration.

However, in thinking about how we engage with Afrikaans as black people, it is important to think through the history of Afrikaans and how it impacts us and the descendants of the Cape slaves, for a more nuanced engagement with the language to happen.

Tsotsis and Tsotsitaal

Tsotsitaal is called a slang by many, a dialect by some. Dr Ellen Hurst of sociolinguistics proposes that it be called a 'stylect'; that is, that the language is accompanied by a style exclusive to it. Of course, we know that Tsotsitaal identifies itself as a language. With the word 'taal' being Afrikaans for 'language', it confuses me slightly that there is so much confusion around what to call Tsotsitaal. Dumisani Ntshangase states that because Tsotsitaal has to base itself on another language, it is not quite a language on its own. While I risk sounding like a person who imagines decoloniality to be a chaotic abandoning of all rules, I do want to contend that it is sinister to determine what a language is based on the structures that western linguistics have taught us. Especially when one considers how, essentially, Afrikaans had used Dutch as its base language and added new lexicons.

An important point to remember is that the differing accounts of Tsotsitaal's origins are all linked to criminal activity. A 'tsotsi' translates quite simply in English to a 'thug'. The fifth Urban Dictionary definition of the word 'thug' states, 'As Tupac defined it, a thug is someone who is going through struggles, has gone through struggles and continues to live day by day with nothing for them.' There is no doubt in my mind that the author of this definition was aware of the historical meaning of the word 'thug'. However, criminality plays out differently when one finds oneself in the so-called 'ghetto'. Slabbert and Myers-Scotton tell us that, from their understanding of Tsotsitaal having emerged mainly from the gangsters in the Witwatersrand, the 'criminals' who returned from prison would popularise Tsotsitaal in the township. This is problematised by the fact that there was a system in place which criminalised the mere fact of being black.

The language was not stigmatised because the apartheid government's perception of crime did not mirror that of the black township population. Deumert takes it further to explain that a 'tsotsi', although a (small scale) criminal, was not a figure that only inspired fear but was also a figure of desire, fantasy, politics, poetry and art. As Ntshangase notes, young black children identified with the tsotsi figure more than they did with professionals. This was a deep-seated expression of the desire to escape the conditions that apartheid created, which legislated black people to be submissive in the face of oppression.

The rebellion of the 'tsotsi', the figure who took it all back by force, was the antithesis of what the apartheid government sought to create. The 'tsotsi' was a figure of resistance against the white man's ideas of submission and cheap black labour. Perhaps that was what made 'tsotsis' aspirational. Of course, the rise of kwaito fashioning and language is consistent with this as the word 'kwaito' itself derives from the well-known gang Amakwaito.

Tsotsitaal managed to move away, although not completely, from being understood as the language of criminals, that is, a 'tsotsi's taal'. In *Kwaito Music*, Mohau Motloi says that the language was also used by migrant workers at large. Older musicians have even stated that the language became a language with which people would tip each other off about the arrival of the apartheid regime's police in the township. It became a language of survival.

Tsotsitaal would also eventually become a language of camaraderie not solely associated with criminality. In fact, Hurst articulates this best when she observes: 'Tsotsitaal is aligned across a spectrum of identities and its purpose is more complex than merely an "argot" or language of criminals. It is employed in the constitution of an identity within a particular township cultural space.'

Towards Iscamtho

Perhaps what leads to the misconception that Iscamtho is Tsotsitaal is the fact that it is, in a sense, a 'tsotsi taal' - that is, a language with its history in criminal activity, along with the recurrence of many words from Tsotsitaal in the Iscamtho lexicon. However, when we become aware of how differently based these languages are; it becomes significantly easier to identify which is which.

Furthermore, as Ntshangase writes, Scamtho and Tsotsitaal draw their languages from differing social and historical communities. While Tsotsitaal draws from townships in Western Johannesburg (that is, Sophiatown, Martindale and Alexandra), Scamtho originates from an argot called 'Shalambombo' and draws from Orlando, Pimville, the Eastern Native Township and the Moroka Emergency Camp. Yet the idea that Scamtho is Tsotsitaal has somehow survived.

Tsotsitaal's prevalence, as I briefly touched on earlier, began to decline with apartheid's imposition of Afrikaans as the medium of instructions in schools. Consider again Professor Deumert's contention that Tsotsitaal is 'a form of cultural-linguistic appropriation or even parody. Taking the language of the oppressor and making it one's own [...] Afrikaans, the language of purity, thus became the language of blackness and hybridity.'

Taking this as our basis, it would not be far-fetched to contend that the appeal of Afrikaans deteriorated as it was institutionally enforced, where originally it had been used as a reclamation of agency in Tsotsitaal. The structural imposition of the language upon the black population was thus the stripping away of the little agency that Tsotsitaal speakers had snatched for themselves from the Afrikaans language. So, the appeal of Iscamtho increased and altered the course of communication in the township.

Common identity, multicultural spaces and reclaiming blackness

The racialisation of black people, people who were not always identified by the colour of their skin, created some cultural complications. Multi-ethnic groups were pushed into the same spaces under the banner of blackness. Tsotsitaal symbolises the moment where these people from different ethnic backgrounds began to form a common language on their own terms. Using Afrikaans, a language imposed upon them, while abandoning many of the rules of the white man's Afrikaans to construct this black identity, was nothing short of rebellion. In our engagement with Afrikaans it is therefore important that we consider its history and think about how we choose to move forward.

When the apartheid government decided to interfere with this process of linguistic appropriation and reclamation, the township tongue chose once again to renegotiate its terms and gravitated towards another form of autonomous blackness: Scamtho. Ntshangase argues that these languages reflect black people's acceptance of the township as home, even though the apartheid system had designed the spatial system to exploit black bodies for labour while keeping them in peri-urban camps on the periphery – perpetual outsiders. Of course, these two languages, stylects or dialects, whatever we choose to call them, are not embraced by all black people in the township.

There are still people who associate them with criminal activity and condemn their use. However, there is also a generation of people who now unwittingly speak Scamtho, with the inescapable elements of Tsotsitaal embedded in it, and it has become an almost naturalised part of their identity.

VIII

I WEAR WHAT I LIKE: FASHION AND KWAITO
Esinako Ndabeni

CLOTHES ARE A VERY KEY, very complex aspect of African cultures. I do not remember a time in my life where I was not aware of the power of clothes and what they can communicate. As little children being raised by our grandparents in the village, our mothers would come home in December with clothes for us to wear on Christmas Day. It was one of the few occasions during which we could receive new clothes and roam our entire village, knocking on people's doors, asking for Christmas goodies. It was always a grand time of year because we were not used to getting new clothes.

Fashion is an instrument to communicate personal, race, class, gender and identity politics. In the West, fashion has, for the most part, been used to police the gender identities that people have; constantly reinforcing the gender binary of 'man' and 'woman'. While women can wear pants without being condemned in most parts of today's western-influenced societies, the reverse is not true for men. There is still a great deal of stigma attached to men dressing the way that women have been socialised into dressing (dresses, skirts, etc). These ideas stem from hegenomic patriarchy's need to always depict a cis-gender heterosexual man as masculinely as possible, and so the idea is that women's clothing emasculates him.

Fashion, in this sense, clearly reinforces the violent ideas that society has about gender. Fashion, like power, is everywhere. It is a politic that we all participate in when we choose to fashion ourselves (or when the fashion is chosen for us). Although casual, the kwaito generation was very deliberate about the clothes they chose to wear. When I asked Spikiri how it is that he dresses ever so modestly, he stated that the people he hung around were not wealthy or flashy people, so he wouldn't want to make them feel small by being flashy.

It goes without saying that fashion has a monumental relationship with capitalism. This is irrefutable in the scandals about multinational corporations using child labour or creating unfair working conditions for their employees (e.g the notorious sweatshops in the East owned by premium labels from the West). It is also clearly evident in the unaffordability of clothes for many in today's 'civilised' world. The relationship between fashion and capitalism is deep. In this essay I want to explore the ways in which fashion has been used in the South African context by both oppressor and oppressed.

Firstly, I hope to bring across how humanity was denied blue-collar workers by the colonial and apartheid regimes.

Secondly, I will attempt to make visible the invisible and dehumanised, subjects of South Africa's history.

Thirdly, and most importantly, I will explore how fashion has been used and deployed by the youth in the period emerging from legislated apartheid.

I WEAR WHAT I LIKE: FASHION AND KWAITO

Shame, man: The blue-collar uniform

Capitalism has done a greatly ingenious job of determining which kind of labour will be most strenuous and therefore least valuable. Black bodies have been tasked with the most physically and emotionally demanding jobs and yet at the same time been convinced that their's are the most menial – tasks undeserving of dignified compensation. In today's society we are constantly told (most stubbornly and and notoriously in recent times by the Twitter rants of one Helen Zille of the Democratic Party) that the country's infrastructure is the beneficial legacy of colonialism, and very seldom do we sit in buildings and think, 'Our ancestors built this'. Even though we all know full well that black labour built this country.

There is no question about the extent to which black labour is completely underappreciated and under compensated. In Marikana on 16 August 2012, mine workers were shot dead (34 dead, 78 wounded), and scores more arrested for protesting for better pay. There was much public scoffing about why manual labourers with little or no formal education could think they could ever be deserving of a R12 500 per month salary. This was yet another testament to the manufactured insignificance of the working class under capitalism, despite their being the engine room that drives and sustains it.

Just in case society is unable to identify these exploited bodies, uniforms are prescribed for them. In the book *Was It Something I Wore?* Sithabile Ntombela, a senior lecturer at the University of KwaZulu-Natal (UKZN) argues that it is not that clothes degrade blue-collar workers (her analysis focuses purely on domestic workers), but rather that these uniforms '[publicise] their position which has been constructed as low in the social order'. It seems to me however that the distinction Ntombela draws is very blurry, because one can argue that by communicating these worker's position in society, these very clothing items degrade those who are made to wear them. From the domestic worker's suit to the blue overalls, blue-collar uniforms have been used as markers of position in society; creating and recreating hierarchies in this way.

While Ntombela's stance (that these uniforms do not degrade those who wear them) is clearly not made with the same intention to aid and abet the degradation of workers, one can see how her argument could be used to justify the forcing of working-class people into these uniforms in ways that lack a nuanced understanding of the effects thereof. It is often said that a uniform attracts neither shame nor pride. It just is. Police officers wear uniforms, domestic workers wear uniforms and that's that. It is just bigoted people who bring their perceptions and experiences to bear in any attaching of meaning to the apparel.

However, when one considers the relationship that poverty has with shame, it becomes clear that this is a short-sighted justification which ignores the role that fashion plays as a tool in communicating prestige (or lack thereof). Furthermore these uniforms identify people as poor, thereby identifying them with a power deficit which is very expressive in materialist capitalism. The *publicising* role that these uniforms play cannot be separated from the *degrading* role that they play. One has to question what it means to publicise one's source of shame: poverty, a lack of education and all the other sources of shame that [working class] black people have to carry.

Reclaiming the blue-collar worker's uniform

In 2014, the Economic Freedom Fighter's (EFF) parliamentarians entered the August House of legislature dressed in their red manual-labour overalls and domestic worker uniforms, like blue-collar workers. Their position was that they were doing this to represent, down to their apparel, the very people who had voted them into parliament. The EFF's use of these clothes, especially in a space where the conventions of dress are so formal and classed, immediately signalled their arrival as a politically significant symbol of black working class solidarity.

It was a radical act of self-identification with the lower rungs of society; validating domestic workers and manual labourers in a symbolic but undeniably powerful way.

Furthermore, what this statement did was that it represented a repurposing of the black working-class persona and narrative. Here were domestic worker uniforms and the overalls of construction site daka-boys (cement mixers) – ever markers for those forced into subservient and subordinate roles – sitting in parliament and contributing to law-making, as Alude Mahali points out in the paper *Maid to Serve: 'Self-Fashioning' and the Domestic Worker Trope.*

One clearly sees in the example of the EFF the power clothing can have as a statement in society, communicating resistance and bringing to light the chasms and ironies that exist. However, well before the EFF donned these uniforms, amapantsula were doing so.

Due to the time period and conditions that it was conceived under, ispantsula as a culture expressed identities that black people forged for themselves after being forcibly removed from their original homes and squeezed into Spartan, insanitary, peri-urban enclaves. Initially, amapantsula's dress sense was deeply inspired by American style: zoot suits and Stetson hats.

There is a certain romanticism with which we view African-Americans from the movies that we have watched. Professor Yvonne Bynoe notes in her article about global hip hop that South Africans revered African-Americans for their braggadocio. Perhaps it has always been a way for us to escape our own misery at home and live out, albeit briefly, a different reality from the one we are caught up in.

As Bogatsu writes, overseas influences became an expression by black South Africans of their rejection of the life that apartheid imposed on them. In terms of fashion, some of the brands popular among amapantsula were Pringle, Brentwood, Florsheim and Saxone. However, these brands were too expensive and inaccessible for the youth and they resorted to styling their school uniforms and adopting workwear as casual dress, ushering in a new era in the popular dress code of amapantsula. This was an interesting shift from the more debonair style of, for example, the main protagonist figure who wrapped the suit he was stealing from a clothes store around his legs and smoothed his pants down before casually walking out in the movie *Mapantsula*.

The ispantsula wave seems to have further confirmed the shifts which saw things that were associated with criminality forming subcultures that people were proud to identify with; Tsotsitaal, ispantsula, and, further on, kwaito as we argue in this book… Furthermore, for all its illusions and disillusions, post-apartheid South Africa has at least enabled black people from both townships and rural areas to be somewhat proud of their identities.

To echo Bogatsu, it is worth noting that after the end of institutionalised apartheid the 'rainbow nation' emerged and with it, the asserting of one's black identity became a more 'fashionable' thing to do, as it fit right in with ideas of the diversity of the new nation. Dressing in the clothes of blue-collar workers and doing dances which depicted the life lived in the township arguably became something more celebratory than it had originally been.

It is unclear whether the decision of artists such as Trompies and Mzekezeke to emerge wearing overalls was a deliberate stance against respectability politics and a communication of the socioeconomic struggles that they had been exposed to. It is highly unlikely that they were unaware of the power that these uniforms had (and continue to have). When we interviewed Spikiri, he was clear in emphasising that kwaito was about the South African black township identity. It was about taking pride in who they are.

In this way, beyond embracing oneself as part of a rainbow, the decision to be artists who dressed like that represents the attempt of many black people to reclaim pre-existing narratives of blackness and poverty. Here were these artists wearing the shame of their parents, their grandparents and their forebears with no shame. In Mzekezeke's case, this repurposing went even deeper. Mzekezeke wore orange overalls and accessorised his look with a balaclava. Mzekezeke's orange overalls were similar to those worn by prisoners, and the balaclava face-concealing headgear is commonly favoured by burglars.

Perhaps he merely wore his balaclava to maintain the sense of mystery which kept his audience guessing, talking. The artist behind the alias 'Mzekezeke' was aware of this public fascination with uncovering his real identity, and even capitalised on it with his hit song *Ubani uMzekezeke* (Who is Mzekezeke?). Whatever the reason, his 'prisoner look' invoked images in the minds of audiences that saw him identified as 'shady'. Mzekezeke was drawing inspiration from the criminalisation of black identity, just as kwaito artists had done from the start, when they named the genre after an old gang called Amakwaito.

The relationship that Black South Africans have with incarceration is a complicated one due to the deliberate and often indiscriminate jailing of black people by previous governments. The conditions of systemic, racialised poverty undoubtedly facilitated the resort to criminal activity. It is therefore undeniable that drawing on images of jailed black persons became a political statement of resistance and solidarity. Knee-jerk reactions which lead to shunning people who embrace the 'prisoner look' as a fashion statement and aesthetic, miss the opportunity to have honest conversations about how a particular history of policing has impacted black bodies.

Perhaps the use of these uniforms of black degradation by kwaito artists may not have been perceived as being as radical as that of the EFF, because the space that they operated within was not as rigid as parliament; especially considering the point I made earlier about how amapantsula started to wear these clothes because of not affording brands such as Brentwood, Saxone etc. However, I would contend that the celebration of self, especially a poor and black self, must always be understood as radical. To actively wear clothes associated with being poor, uneducated and criminal, could not have been anything other than radical.

It is a rejection of the negative baggage that is projected upon people who, by force of circumstance, have to dress that way. I would argue that this is so even when it is not done with the conscious desire to actively politicise. These overalls and uniforms must be understood as an ode to migrant labour, a tribute and reclaiming of toiling, degraded, discarded black bodies. Black bodies whose physical work is the glue that holds society together.

Even besides their work overalls, the clothes kwaito artists generally chose to wear made a loud statement, disrupting society's ideas of how one should present oneself. Subsequently, these artists were notoriously known as 'amavuilpop', who were essentially undeserving of respect. This sentiment is questionable just when one considers who gets to construct morality (hint: the wealthy and powerful).

Disregarding these notions of propriety in dress, pushing back against preconceived prejudices, kwaito artists unapologetically wore their Converse All Stars, Dickies apparel, overalls and 'is'poti' (bucket hat). With regard to 'is'poti', debate has raged in recent times around who decides when it is a bucket hat and when it is is'poti, highlighting how modern-day politics of class make for complex relations within black culture. It is from such contexts and contests that Loxion Kulca emerged in 1999.

Loxion Kulca: Pioneering post-apartheid streetwear

Sechaba Mogale was born in exile in Lusaka, Zambia, where he was raised by his grandparents, while Wandi Nzimande was born and raised in Soweto. They forged a friendship and went on to create the brand Loxion Kulca in 1997. The wordplay of the 'Loxion' in the brand's name is that it is a stylistic take on the vernacular word for the township, 'elok'shini' (location). 'Kulca' follows this stylisticly, respelling the word 'culture'. Nzimande explains:

> For me, apart from poetic licence: being brave, being young and saying, 'fuck it, we can do whatever we want', we knew that we couldn't spell it in a way that... We knew that if you call it something that people knew, they wouldn't buy it. We wanted to be as foreign as possible because, for me, anything that is foreign instils fear. And, sometimes, fear instils respect. So, we were excited about the misspelling.

The brand Loxion Kulca was a representation of the cultures that these designers were exposed to. Nzimande and Mogale had started out by selling handmade t-shirts and caps from the boot of their car. They then approached Sales House, known today as Jet Stores, part of the Edgars Consolidated Stores (EDCON). Sales House had started off as a retail clothing store tailored to the interests of migrant labourers. Sales House sold clothes similar to the Brentwoods and Pringles favoured by amapantsula, but at more affordable rates and with extended credit. Edgars was catering to middle class white people at the time.

Mogale and Nzimande approached Sales House with the desire to become a vendor at the store, and one of the EDCON's suppliers, the late Brian Abrahams, assisted them financially and became their business partner. The period being just after apartheid, the market was incredibly difficult for black people to enter, and Abrahams's social and economic capital came in handy for the duo. Loxion Kulca became one of the vendors at Sales House stores, but unfortunately the brand didn't sell very well in the first week, which is usually used to measure how well a product will perform on the market. It was not until they got kwaito artists to endorse the brand that the sales for Loxion Kulca skyrocketed. From there, Loxion Kulca rose to prominence as a brand celebrating the township identity using streetwear. Not long after its inception Loxion Kulca began to be worn by major kwaito artists such as Mshoza and TKZee. After the death of business partner, Brian Abrahams, the brand then seemed to lose prominence and momentum due to a series of reasons. One major reason given by Nzimande was that, in its popularity, the brand had created such great demand for the products that they were unable to meet required supply. Largely because of this, counterfeiting of their brand increased drastically. At one stage, he recounted for the Sowetan newspaper, there was R10-million worth of bootlegged Loxion Kulca products being sold on the streets.

Loxion Kulca, and Wandi Nzimande agrees with me on this, owed a great deal of its success to the kwaito movement, becoming something of a symbol for the culture. Needless to say, as kwaito left the mainstream, Loxion Kulca followed suit as the genre had facilitated and championed its success. Whatever other reasons may have led to the brand's decline, it is undeniable that Loxion Kulca paved the way for streetwear brands such as Amakipkip, Eish Hade and the Cape Town based 2Bop. Izipoti (bucket hats) have especially made their way into mainstream streetwear today, propelled even more following the video of Caracara released by KO ft KiDX in 2013, which paid homage specifically to Trompies but to kwaito as a genre and a culture as well.

The song sampled Trompies's popular hit *Bengimngaka*, and the artists wore bucket hats and even made reference to TKZee's 1998 hit, *Dlala Mapantsula*. The fact that bucket hats have made their way back into the mainstream through hip hop is quite profound. Whether deliberate or not, this move highlights the way in which our identities today, as black people living in post-apartheid South Africa but also in the global village, are not as rigid as we like to make them out to be. Is'poti, or the bucket hat, signals that there is a bridge between two different cultures that young black South Africans find themselves grappling with today. Loxion Kulca's brilliance was also in the brand's ability to remix history, so to speak. The contemporary youth, just post-apartheid, struggled to place or limit themselves in one cultural space, as this was also around the time when globalisation's effects became more pronounced on South African society. The first post-apartheid generation could not escape the politics of its past, and yet also sought to find a different identity from the apartheid generations.

Loxion Kulca clothing and gear was not necessarily traditionally township; influences from black American fashion were also prevalent. In fact, Wandi Nzimande and Sechaba Mogale had been people who prided themselves on being fans of hip hop and were also avid basketball players, so this fact shouldn't be surprising. However, for all its attached sentimental and political meanings, Wandi Nzimande is on record stating that the brand was not born out of some special story to tell, and instead came out of their need to put bread on the table. 'To us it was a means to an end while to some people it gave them belief, and others created music with it. Some people even thought we were a political party,' he once recounted for City Press.

Without imposing an unintended meaning, I would say that many of the actions that we make do not necessarily have one meaning. A lot of times, they are in response to actions that have already been made. If we interrogated further, we would find that many of our most significant actions are informed by the world around us.

Fashion, like all other art forms, can also be used as a window to seeing and making meaning out of the experiences that people have of a certain time and place, even when that was not the explicit meaning of the designer. The name 'Loxion Kulca' in a South Africa where black people were still trying to figure out where they fit in the world is political in itself, as it shows pride in being from elok'shini, a place which was supposed to be the site of hopelessness. The clothing, reflecting the black South African township experience even as it had been influenced by global super-culture, reflected the one thing that black folks cannot be stripped of: our identities.

Things were slightly different for female kwaito artists, however. Because my engagement with kwaito is with hindsight, as I was a young child when the culture was prominent, there are many things that hold sentimental value to me. Boom Shaka wearing crop tops that were perceived as revealing, for example. Boom Shaka's style, clearly influenced by African-American fashion even through its music, was critiqued for how 'loose' an image it portrayed. This was an aesthetic that even 999's Abashante followed. The women were clad in revealing tops and long pants as it was the trend at the time, imported from black America.

Considering the role that men played in creating these images, I struggle to think of them as bold attempts at reclaiming their agency. I can't shake off the feeling that the kwaito men instructed them to cultivate these images, specifically for the male gaze. It is difficult to engage with the clothing style of kwaito artists without engaging with South Africa's sociopolitical dynamics. At all times, it was about confronting respectability politics. It serves as a window into the socio-political climate of neo-apartheid South Africa, where apartheid is no longer legislated but remains stubbornly reflected in the socioeconomics of its people. The fashion and culture kwaito style ignited paved the way for our generation to be able to express ourselves through unconventional modes of dress, and will live on forever as an inspiration to us.

IX

TKZee: Amapantsul' ajabulile
Sihle Mthembu

In 2015 neuroscientists and psychologists in Middletown, Connecticut did a study on the links between music and physical reactions. Having analysed the effects of dozens of songs in closed-ended experiments conducted over a year, they concluded that there is an inextricable link between what the ear hears and how the rest of the senses and the body react. According to Professor Psyche Loui, who was one of the lead researchers on the project, music can trigger messages to the brain that can lead to physical reactions as powerful as orgasms. The phenomenon is called frisson and is also known as a skin orgasm. Reactions can include trembling, sweating, tingling and even arousal.

The study, which was conducted in conjunction with Wesleyan University, cost over $30 000 dollars. If Professor Loui and her team had been to a street bash in South Africa during the late 1990s when any TKZee track from their album *Halloween* came on, they could have saved themselves some money and confirmed what South African youth had long since already known.

You had to have been there. Of course this is what we writers tell our readers to try and convince them that our past was better than their present. But this time believe me, it's true: you had to have been there. If you were born sometime before 1994 you've probably had the experience I'm talking about. The sudden gasp followed by an elongated squeal which, if someone doesn't understand what's happening, might cause them to rush to your side to help or to calm you, to grab hold of your hand and ask if you're okay. But those who were there knew.

They knew that they were in the presence of the ultimate expression of black joy 'eating its youth' (a literal translation from the isiZulu, 'sidl'ubusha bethu' (to thoroughly enjoy ones youth). The elaborate, vigorous hand signals. The lasciviously stuck-out tongue. This was the mass physical effect when the strings would come on around 30 seconds into TKZee's *Mambotjie*. I've seen it so often, yet it still gets me every time.

I meet Kabelo at Vovo Telo, an eatery located on the side of a small mart in Sandton. Here they serve artisan coffee, smoothies, and overpriced sandwiches that taste like punk rock. I find it hard to believe that this is where the man who sang 'Ngilipantsula for life' now spends his mornings. 'Bouga Luv', as Kabelo is famously known by his legions of fans, is clearly a regular here. The waiters and owner know him by name, and some of the patrons stop to greet. In the two hours that we spend chatting, quite a few people having breakfast greet him from a distance. He smiles magnanimously and waves back to all of them without ever whispering under his breath about how he hates being disturbed. Kabelo should not be so gracious. Both of us have suddenly been drained by the news of Bra Hugh's passing. So, sitting here and talking about kwaito seems as frivolous and yet as important as ever.

He is carrying a sling bag, sporting red Nike sneakers and a red vest, having come straight from an intense morning gym session. Personal fitness is something he's into now, in addition to preaching the word of God at Rhema. Both are attempts, in all probability, at rebuilding a body and spirit that years of kwaito, alcohol, life on the road and hard drugs almost wrecked. He tells me that, as an extension of his healthy living plan, he intends to open up a health-food shop not too far from where we are seated. 'It's gonna be a few blocks up the road. I found a business partner and we are going to create a space where people can have access to food and things that will help them heal their bodies and be healthy. It's an exciting project and is hopefully gonna help people take their lives back.'

Kabelo isn't very interested in music these days; not even in talking about it, let alone making it. In fact he wasn't even sure about doing this interview. He tells me that when he was younger he used to buy every album as soon as it came out and analyse it over and over, but that now he's more of a passive listener. 'I remember we (TKZee) used to be such music nerds; we had every album and it would be like we would compete to see who heard it first. We listened to everything, all the time. Then we would come to the studio and talk about it for hours on end.'

It is this keen appetite and gluttonous consumption that created the colours in TKZee's musical pallet: the flashy string sections, the mixed tempo drums, the understated synths. All the (sometimes unlikely, always refreshing) elements of it come from the different references they had as music listeners first before they transitioned into music-makers, as Kabelo explains:

> A lot of what we made came about as a reaction to what we were listening to. Especially around the time of our album, *Halloween*, because in music you are influenced by what you like and what you don't, so often there were cases where we wanted to do certain things and try certain sounds but it didn't work out. Being such avid consumers of music, we could always hear when things felt and sounded forced.

The more you talk to the members of TKZee about the construction of *Halloween* the more one thing becomes clear, there wasn't a grand plan. A flu-ridden Zwai, fresh off the run of *Tsotsi: The Musical*, also tells me about the difficulty of recording the album in a constant state of transition.

> We had a deadline for the record but there wasn't any real moment where we sat down and talked and plotted what we were trying to do. We were constantly making music, and eventually we had to sit down with the sketches that we had and try to develop them into songs that we could use for the record. There was also a lot of stuff left over that we planned to use, but it just didn't fit the mood of the album.

TKZee used a heightened understanding of musical structure and a keen ear for instrumentation as a springboard to creating an album that was musically superior to most of the stuff coming out at the time, but also to do a kind of bait and switch. Whilst the majority of the lyrics on the record are upbeat and whimsical, there are deeper, darker shades that underpin it all. Fear of alienation from one's community is what drives the narrative arc of the album. The nine-track offering, for that is what it is; an offering, an attempt to thank the ancestors and the living not only for their success but for everything that came with it. As Zwai points out, they had come from being nobodies to being millionaires in a matter of months, after the back to back successes of *Phalafala* and *Shibobo*.

> We knew that we had to document that transition and everything that came with it. Mostly good, but also the bad. The music itself was also just a form of therapy and a way of adjusting to the spotlight,' he says. 'See we suddenly had all these fans and everything we'd ever wanted, and so being in studio was great because it allowed us to feel like we were still us.

At the time that TKZee made *Halloween* they were also

listening to a lot of jazz. They were frequent faces at that Sodom and Gomorrah of jazz joints in Jozi called The Bassline. It was around this time that Kabelo met Moses Taiwa Molelekwa, and the two of them struck up a friendship that stretched beyond the confines of music. 'I had one of his albums and one day I saw him out on the street. I got out of the car and rushed to ask him to sign it and he did. From there we just became close friends, and he was really one of the people who supported us a lot and appreciated what we were doing,' he recalls.

Plans for Moses to work on some music with the trio were long in the making, and he did eventually, giving Kabelo some music for the latter's own solo albums, as well as TKZee's *GUZ 2001* project, before his untimely and mysterious death. 'He could hear things in our music that even we couldn't hear. That is how heightened his spirit was, and I think just knowing people like him were around and pushing boundaries made us want to go further outside of our comfort zones musically.'

Halloween kicks off with *Come*, an experimental intro whose drum kick patterns seem closer to trap now than anything you might have heard in kwaito back then. The beat builds and with each loop new instruments and kicks are added until almost the two minute mark, when it feels ripe for a good beat-switch and a verse which never comes. Just as the music reaches a crescendo, the experience ends. What this intro does is what any good intro should do: set you up both sonically and emotionally for what the rest of the album has to say. That intro told us that these guys weren't here to play by the rules.

'1998 was such a busy year for us but we stopped doing everything for two weeks so we could work on this album. I didn't want to limit myself and I just let the spirituality of the music flow,' says Zwai. 'That's why you hear big, layered orchestral arrangements in there, because I didn't want to compromise on that vision,' he tells me. *Halloween* came out at a time when the American holiday was more obscure in South Africa than it is now. It was also at the peak of South Africa's 'rainbow-nationism', before the libation got too strong or too weak and a devastating hangover set in. It feels like a long way away now. Of the time Zwai says:

> It was a very happy time and place in 1998. The kind of partying that used to happen was on another level. We were really enjoying the feeling of freedom, and whatever we were dreaming about, we could actually see it happening. So *Halloween* was a response to that; the record represented the kind of unfiltered happiness we saw around us daily.

TKZee had a few advantages already in place before the release of *Halloween* which allowed them to craft this classic on a solid foundation. Behind them was the team at BMG Africa, who were notorious for their hands-off approach to urban music, which meant the artists could do whatever they wanted from a creative standpoint. The backing team at BMG were mainly involved with marketing and distribution. 'We were the first kwaito act signed to BMG,' recalls Zwai. 'So they didn't really know how to deal with us and because we had our own set up and our overheads were so low, they really just left us alone to make music. Nobody ever came into the studio and asked to see what we were working on until the album was turned in.'

TKZee also had, at this point, the experience of both failure and success and had picked up a few good friends along the way. You might not know this but 1997's *Phalafala* wasn't the group's first studio production. In fact, in 1996 they had dropped the EP *Take it Eezy*, an obscure early offering which the trio released under their own TKZee Rekordz, featuring just four tracks. Listening to it now, you hear flashes of brilliance, from Magesh with his signature, stop-start flow and cadence to Zwai's harmonies and Kabelo's effortless wit. This was a group still very much at the inception of its identity, and as a result the project bombed.

'We were still young guys really unsure about what we were doing and what we wanted to say,' Tokollo tells me over the phone.

'I think we learned a lot from the album about how to collaborate with each other. It also forced us to refine our sound and rethink how we could take the hip hop influence and make it work in a South African context.'

This is where the part about good friends comes in. At their lowest point, with the EP having bombed, the band turned to Sbu, who at the time was piping hot. Sbu was already friends with Magesh from their time at Mashamplani, and also knew Kabelo and Zwai. He would serve as a kind of sage and guiding voice to the trio as they worked on their next offerings, *Phalafala* and later *Halloween*.

'Sbu was always the guy that told us to just be ourselves. I think a lot of people were making music that at times felt realy inauthentic and not reflective of who they were. Sbu encouraged us to talk about our lives and what we knew,' says Tokollo. Another profoundly influential person on the sound of *Halloween* was Godfrey 'Guffy' Pilane, who at the time was very close friends with Zwai.

'He was someone I was inspired by even outside of his musical expertise, by just the way his mind used to work. He had a scientific approach to music and he is the guy that really picked me up at the prime of his hit-making, and taught me that not everything in music is about music,' Zwai says. Pilane recalls hearing some of the rough drafts of the music for *Halloween* in his studio with Zwai and being perplexed and intrigued by the group's sound:

> The thing that people don't understand is how much music went into making that album. I remember Zwai playing the album for me and by about the fifth track I knew that this wasn't something ordinary. These guys were literally about to change the history of South African music and they didn't even realise it, they were just being themselves. Most people never get to that level of talent.

By the time *Halloween* came around TKZee's sampling had become a hallmark of the band's sound. This created a cosmic shift in the soundscape of kwaito music that can never be undone. From Joni Mitchell's *Big Yellow Taxi* in *Phalafala* to Madonna's *Papa Don't Preach* in *Fella Kae*, TKzee's samples were not just about taking a hit, repackaging it over a slowed down beat, reciting some catchy phrases over it and sending it out to sea. Instead, they sampled strictly to enhance what was already happening in the song, rather than to cover up mediocrity. Their sampling was not without purpose; it was both ethereal and instinctive.

For *Halloween*, however, they had to shed this old skin in an attempt to create something completely new; a world of their own that still retained the big arrangements they were attracted to. They were deliberately selective and often found that samples were not the way to go for some of the tracks on the album. 'The thing people don't understand is that when you hear a song, you think it might work for a sample then you use it. You don't first have music and then try hunt for samples to make up for what is not working on the record. That is not music-making,' argues Zwai.

What makes *Halloween* work so well is that the 10-track album is lean and full of purpose, but the music is also very indulgent. Most of the songs run for more than four and a half minutes, some of them go up to six, and yet the lengthier cuts do not meander. The party begins on *Magesh*, with Zwai's love for strings meeting Tokollo's knack for repeated, offbeat phrasing. *Magesh* is a good entry point because it sounds like a raw, more libatious extension of *Shibobo*, which had been released with Benni McCarthy a few months before *Halloween*.

'Phakamis' izandla zakho laph' ukhona, uz'veze, sik'bone' (Throw your hands in the air where you are, show yourself so we can see you), rasps Tokollo. A phrase that at one time could have struck fear in the hearts of black people, living as they did under an oppressive system where survival often depended on becoming invisible, now plays out as a call for redemption on the dance floor.

'For me, when I write I try and keep it personal but also make it relatable. I bring the language of the streets into every verse because personal encounters are so important to me. Connections with people drive everything I do in my music, so I try to give back the inspiration that has been given to me,' says Tokollo.

You don't need me to tell you that *Dlala Mapantsula* is one of the standout tracks on this record, hell it's arguably one of the best songs TKZee ever made. Everything they stood for encapsulated in 6:10 minutes of anthemic madness. But what you might not have noticed is how jazzy the structure of the grooves is on this motherfucker. Where most kwaito tracks coasted along on looping, with maybe a verse and a chorus, TKZee broke with that tradition completely.

Around the 1:20 minute mark, the song, which has up to that point been an ensemble of strings, drowns all of them out. A synthetized loop rises in the background and the strings change, and by the two-minute mark, when those celestial strings come back, they move at a different pace, aided along by the kick. They continue to disappear and re-emerge in slightly different incarnations throughout the song. The holding phrase of *Dlala Mapantsula* also feels slightly more ominous the second time Tokollo comes around.

Sikelela is arguably the weakest song on the offering, which is saying a lot about the project's strength when a song which influenced so much of South African slang for the next three years is your album's Achilles' heel. The word 'sikelela' appropriated our national anthem and would itself later be appropriated by AKA on *Run Jozi*, to much better effect I'd say, but that's a conversation for another day. Speaking of appropriating, most people actually don't realise that Kabelo's *Reverse Yomhlaba* was actually a reference to a line from Magesh's verse on *Sikelela*. On the original joint however, Zwai flexes his vocal skills and shows off his arrangements at their most ambitious by layering his voice to sound like a choir. Why then despite all this is Zwai still so dissatisfied with this whole album? He's at pains to explain it:

> I knew we had something special and I didn't want to fuck it up. I even fell ill around the mixing and finalizing of the

album because of the pressure. I just wish I had more time to perfect it. To really explore and expand the ideas that we had there. I mean people don't know that those aren't the final versions of *Mambotjie* and *We Love This Place*. A lot of the record sometimes feels like really good first drafts to me, but hey, people still love it.

Kabelo also wishes they'd had more time, but not necessarily to perfect the album. 'I think we rushed the rollout,' he says. '*Halloween* has lived for years but at the time we released it, the singles did well, the album sold and we were on to the next and doing shows. I wish we'd fully exploited the commercial side of that record.'

I find myself in Pretoria and the town seems so small. Convenience stores and everything crammed together in a kind of deliberate claustrophobia. Pretoria is trash. An attempt at keeping the city in place as more and more each day, here in the capital, the evidence suggests that the center is refusing to hold. This is also the town where, in three days, I learn a lot about kwaito. Perhaps more than I'd like to. We are driving back from the National Library where the silence seems like a time warp. Where my co-author and I had sat on high chairs for days, scavenging old copies of *DRUM*, *Next* and *Y Magazine* trying to distinguish the facts from the fables.

Esi looks at me like I'm buggin' when I tell her that Magesh is my favourite TKZee member. 'Nobody likes Tokollo,' she says. 'Tokollo is not a thing.' I'm reminded that Esi and I are born eight years apart. What a difference a decade makes! To people my age, Magesh is a god. Before R Mashesha was hailed as an avant-garde lyricist or Professor, he was lauded as an elusive wordsmith. Magesh has been ruling it. In the back of the Uber as we breeze past late afternoon traffic and I imagine the Gautrain ride ahead before I head back to Soweto, I want to tell Esi that Kabelo is great and all but he didn't make *Number 1 Tsotsi*.

I want to tell her that Zwai is a super-producer, one of the most important we have and he must be protected at all costs, but he

TOP AND BOTTOM: *Former Ghetto Ruff musician Bonginkosi Dlamini, better known as Zola, rocks a crowd of South African expats with his song* Ghetto Fabulous *during a club performance in Woolwich, England.*

Top, bottom-left and right: *Arthur Mafokate performing live with 999's groundbreaking girl group, Abashante, at Club Temple in April 2000. Following their debut album, Abashante took South Africa by storm with their progressive and provocative music, outfits and dance routines which were modelled on American girl groups of the mid-90s.*

Top-left: *Bongo Maffin perform live at the Cargo on 5 May 2002.* **Top-right:** *Stoan is the MC in the Afro-centric outfit and is often credited as one of the pioneers of the motswako hip hop sound.* **Bottom-left:** *Thandiswa Mazwai, who was not originally part of the group but joined Speedy, Stoan and Jah Seed after the group released their first album* Leaders of D'gong. **Bottom-right:** *Thandiswa Mazwai also collaborated with bandmate Jah Seed on* Lahl'umlenze, *one of the standout cuts from her solo debut album* Zabalaza.

Top-left: *In one of his more iconic style moments Mandoza rocks a blue velvet tracksuit as he performs with Chiskop at The Temple night club on 30 March 2001.* **Top-right:** *Mdu Masilela, who was one half of MM Deluxe along with Mandla Spikiri before going solo, performs at The Temple night club.* **Bottom-left and right:** *Pop songstress Brenda Fassie along with longtime collaborator Chicco Twala are ancestors of the sound of kwaito and through their up-tempo bubblegum provided a template for township party music.*

Top-left: *Kabelo Mabalane, aka Bouga Luv, made a name for himself as one third of TKZee before going solo and making hits like* Pantsula 4 life *and* Zonke. **Top-right:** *Dr Mageu on stage prior to his conviction on charges of rape. The* Otla Fella Kae *singer died in prison in September 2008.* **Bottom-left:** *Tokollo Tshabalala, aka Magesh, became known for his iconic lyrics and word play on TKZee's* Halloween. **Bottom-centre and right:** *Sbu and Zwai Bala on stage at The Temple night club during the 2001 TKZee family tour of London.*

Top: *TKZee shifted the paradigm of kwaito by drawing from musical influences outside of hip hop and house and using samples.* **Bottom-left:** *Trompies is a group that defined the sound of kwaito in the '90s and among their best-known songs is* Magasman *which featured Lebo Mathosa and sold over 120 000 units.* **Bottom-right:** *Ishmael connects three generations of music through his affiliations to Prophets of Da City, Skeem and Jozi.*

TOP AND BOTTOM: *Eugene, Zayne, Mandla and Jairus as part of Trompies became defining figures of the pantsula movement and were synonymous with the brightly coloured outfits and outrageous dance moves that defined the kwaito lifestyle.*

Top-left: *Brown Dash rose to fame as a songwriter and his breakout album,* Umthandazo Wabolova, *boasted hits like* Phants' Komthunzi Welanga *and* Vum Vum. **Top-right:** *Often controversial, Mzekezeke was one of kwaito music's last big stars and sparked mystery among fans about his true identity as he always performed with a mask on.* **Bottom:** *TS Records headed by DJ Sbu and TK housed acts like Ntando, Brown Dash, Izinyoka and Mzekezeke.*

ain't the one who said, 'Hello, hello December'. But right then I don't have the energy for all that. I'm too worn down by a day of coming across ANC ads which reference kwaito for Mbeki's 1999 election campaign, and dealing with the fact that as late as 1998, *DRUM Magazine* openly referring to Tony Kgoroge in it's pages as a 'kwerekwere' (derogatory term for black African immigrants in South Africa) was still acceptable behaviour.

In the days that follow, Esi's statement haunts me. 'Tokollo is not a thing.' All of the reasons people don't like Magesh almost always have nothing to do with the music. He has been repeatedly charged with assault. One time in 1999, after the group had won a SAMA for best group, Magesh assaulted a 16-year-old woman who also turned out to be the daughter of politician and businessman Tokyo Sexwale. Magesh pleaded guilty. In 2008 he was acquitted in Botswana on charges of reckless driving and causing a death. The accident had taken place in 2001 and for eight years authorities in that country tried to have Tokollo extradited until he decided to stand trial in late 2007.

According to police reports, Magesh had been speeding after they tried to stop him for ignoring a road sign in Mogoditshane village, outside Gaborone. Magesh was pursued by cops before crashing head-on into an oncoming vehicle, leading to the death of the other driver, businesswoman Maria Monyatsi.

'I think, looking back TKZee was never the same after that, because I was never the same. I didn't want to make music. I just fell into a dark hole because everything I was doing and making just didn't come from a good space,' says Magesh. 'How can you make music for people to party to when all you want to do is sit in your house all day and be depressed?'

When Tokollo came back home from Botswana, he wasn't himself. He started drinking more and didn't feel like making music for months. This was when the slow, inevitable decline of TKZee began and never let up. Out of the trio Magesh is the one who has not cultivated a strong personal brand, despite having been at the heart of the group. Kabelo went on to become a solid kwaito legend who is a reformed drug user and now pushes a healthy lifestyle and an anti-crime campaign called Shout. Zwai is the chilled guy in the trio, the one who harmonised a bit more than the other two, and he does gospel, afro-soul and dabbles in musical theatre. Magesh is the genius we forgot. When I ask Kabelo about the different paths the three of them have taken he sighs and tells me things are different now.

'We are not as close as we used to be, that's for sure. Priorities have shifted,' he says. When one is swept up by the emotional whirlwind of listening to *Halloween*, because that is what it is: being moved by a sudden and irresistible wind, we neglect the technical aspects of TKZee's achievements. No, not their multi-platinum, award-winning status. Not the sold-out shows and millions who still worship at the altar of the trio. As an album *Halloween* has passed the ultimate test; time.

At a packed Good Sundae show in Durban, TKZee perform to a crowd half their age who, during the hour-long set, recite every line from every song word for word. It's less of a performance than it is a collaboration. They aren't what they used to be; Magesh's breath control is laboured, Kabelo doesn't seem to be as comfortable moving on stage, and Zwai as always is the guy in the background who only takes center stage during his parts and is most content letting his peers shine. But nobody cares about all that, the crowd is just glad that these guys are still around.

I ask Kabelo why, if the friendship ain't what it used to be, does he still put himself through the agony of performing these songs and these shows? Isn't it painful, to constantly be reminded of how things used to be? He pauses and in his hand gently spins the espresso shot cup which is now empty. 'What can you do? This thing is bigger than us,' he tells me and you know what, he ain't lying. To see TKZee perform *Halloween* live is to look into a mirror. To be enthralled by the beautiful messiness of it.

It would not be a bad idea for South Africans to measure time not as BC or AD but as BH and AH. Before *Halloween* and after

Halloween. Let me take a moment to say this: *Halloween* is not my favourtite kwaito album. Zola's searing paen on the complexity of black-malehood, *Bhambatha*, takes that honour. But *Halloween*'s place is undeniable; it stands head and shoulders above everything as a pure musical and lyrical kwaito masterpiece.

Music teaches us how to be with people. How to not be alone. How easy it is to adjust to happiness. Through *Halloween* TKZee showed young black men and women of my generation how to be with each other in a joyous context. For so long when we came together as a community, our togetherness was underpinned by fear. Black people in large groups tend to induce paranoia. By way of *Halloween* our joy in being young, gifted, black and alive was made valid again. This is why today I still refuse to be disrespected by white people who have never danced to this album. Now, if I could just get Zwai to send me that alternative mix of *We Love This Place* he told me about…

X

Yizo Yizo: The poetry of dysfunction
Sihle Mthembu

'Ekasi we don't wear gloves when we do the dishes,' she says before breaking into laughter, like she just opened the door into a secret inside joke for which only she has the keys. Thembi Seete is a South Africa canon bomb. She's one of the last survivors of kwaito-era cool at its peak. The last woman standing from an entire generation of leather-wearing, Chuck Taylor-stomping sonic insurgents. Right now, however, she is not her commanding Boom Shaka tour-de force self. Not the Thembi we know from pre-Y2K videos as the Thelma to Lebo Mathosa's Louise.

She is seated in her Jozi home, reclined, taking it easy and talking about one of the projects that has defined her almost two-decade long career. 'It's a silly thing to think you can have a show about the township where you have the characters washing the dishes wearing gloves. Our show was a game changer in that it took away silly little things like that. He brought us in and we got into the details and knocked it out of the park every week,' she says, a hint of seriousness breaking through the humourous demeanour

YIZO YIZO: THE POETRY OF DYSFUNCTION

she had just a second ago.

The show in question is *Yizo Yizo*, that once-in-a-generation flag-bearer for a surprisingly South African form of nihilism. The cinematic invasion that, for three seasons dominated our small screens and offered a rare, unfiltered view into the rape, crime, slang and the various template characters that were the bedrock of townships around the country.

The man who Thembi is speaking about and the silent puppeteer behind this show's rock n' roll journey, is Angus Gibson, a medium-sized character who is little known outside of South African TV circles. Safe shoulder-size, not broader than what you'd expect from a braai-eating, camera-wielding, cinematic clairvoyant. He is a smuggler of cultural contraband and the soothsayer of South African paranoia. Gibson is the surprisingly human figure that is the real hero behind this story. His physical presence does not do justice to the weight of his name every time it flashes when the credits roll on local television.

With smooth, thinning white hair that sits just at the shoulders, Gibson is controlled and contemplative. He talks with the kind of self-awareness that can only be mastered by someone who secretly knows something known by nobody else in the room. And it was he who, along with long term partner in crime Teboho Mahlatsi, coordinated the most impressive mess in South African television history. Gibson tells me the story of how the iconic *Yizo Yizo* came to life:

> Teboho and I had been writing a vigorous, funny but wild feature called *Streetbash*, set in the basement of a downtown building. Our partner, Isaac Shongwe, who was unnerved by *Streetbash's* nihilism, suggested that we do something more constructive and pitch for an educational drama which SABC 1 was commissioning. We agreed that we would do it on the side. We put together a team of interesting people, none of whom had written or worked in television drama before. Teboho

and myself were from documentary backgrounds. Peter Esterhuysen had written textbooks and comics. Mtutuzeli Matshoba had written short stories and Harriet Perlman had edited *Upbeat,* a youth magazine. We started assembling ideas in the downtown basement, sticking cards on the walls. We assumed it would take just a few months of our lives. It ended up consuming most of the next seven years.

The Laduma Film Factory (As Bomb Productions was then known) won the bid and was given carte blanche to create a TV series that addressed education issues in schools. But the program that came out of what was a relatively straightforward brief, was both necessary and otherworldly. Set partially around Supatsela High School, the show dives into the depths of the education system and the effect a broken-down school system can have on its surrounding community. *Yizo Yizo* is a visual poem. The show's first season is an elegy to the death of hope and the need to face up earnestly to the cancerous uncertainties that were eating away at our rainbow nation dream. The most surprising thing about watching the show now is how well it holds up. Its themes of desparate youth, communal collapse and social uncertainty are as relevant now as they were when the series first hit the small screen. Gibson reflects:

> It set out to draw attention to the crisis in the township schools and I think it was successful in that, although some people suggested that the crisis was heightened by *Yizo Yizo* itself. In the context of local black television that had gone before, people were mixing language for the first time, using slang, swearing. The more experienced members of the crew were often horrified by what was happening in front of the camera. The style and the content broke many rules that they believed were sacred. Again and again young people were saying that they were seeing themselves reflected on the screen for the first time.

YIZO YIZO: THE POETRY OF DYSFUNCTION

Despite the fact that The Bomb Shelter Film & Television Production Company has gone on to create interesting content in the form of shows like *Zone 14, Isibaya* and *Isethembiso, Yizo Yizo* continues to be their magnus opus. It has been studied by academics and lionised township Iscamtho. More than a decade after the last episode was aired the SABC, in its usual scramble for relevance, has reverted to re-screening the series, repeatedly airing late-night reruns of the seminal program. These are all merely the byproducts of making a show that canonised a moment.

Perhaps it's bad form in journalism to talk about your own experience in a story, but indulge me for a moment. It's worth mentioning that for the so-called Generation X, South Africans who came of age in Mbeki-era Mzansi, *Yizo Yizo* was the first taste of a thing going 'viral'. I remember skipping school with my friends and catching a rerun of the episode that had Ronnie Nyakale's Papa Action being sodomised in prison by Nongoloza played by Israel Mokae. If you were young, black and 'with it' in ekasi, you did not experience the early 2000s properly unless you had at least one copy of *Yizo Yizo* taped via VCR, which you would play with your friends when the parentals were away.

Watching the show back then was a hyper-real experience bordering on the surreal. With its awkward angles and extreme close-ups, zooming into faces sweaty with the Daveyton heat, it felt like a hallucinogen-induced dream every time. But it wasn't. It was just Gibson and his township requiem strumming their guitars and cameras for a cinematic nightmare. Blackness had never been framed so closely, so terrifyingly, so beautifully. It felt both like baptism and drowning. About the approach to narrative and cinematography they chose to use Gibson says:

> At the time we were very influenced by Asian cinema (Wong Kar-wai and Satyajit Ray), and shows like *Homicide* – all of which explored the handheld camera and had an honest kind of documentary feel. We were of the opinion

that the 'Rainbow Nation' was a con. Our nation was in an extraordinarily aggressive moment and we were not acknowledging it in the media. We wanted to provide what we thought was a more honest view.

Sthandiwe Kgoroge was one of the first people cast for the show, and went on to win an Avati award for her role as Miss Cele, the eternally optimistic new teacher who finds herself thrust into the mess that is Supatsela High. The accomplished actress says she thinks that the reason *Yizo Yizo* hit home was because of the production team that was behind it, as much as it was due to the courage of the cast to get in front of the story. *Yizo Yizo* was ground-breaking for South African television.

'I sincerely believe we need more dramas like that; stories which don't sugarcoat reality and give the youth a false sense of what is happening. The SA industry needs to stop being so PC,' Sthandiwe says, sounding slightly irked by the humdrum of it all. 'I played a pretty straight forward character and I didn't really get any funny reactions from audiences, just encouragement. But what I missed most about being on that set was the energy. Everyone there was excited about what we were doing, therefore we gave our best,' she adds.

Part of Gibson's genius is a Steve Jobs kind of thing. He has Jedi mastery in surrounding himself with people that are infinitely talented; some perhaps much more than he. Mthuthuzeli Matshoba was easily one of the more inspired choices. A short, stoutly built man with the weather-beaten smile of an activist and an almost roundish belly, he seems like a father figure for both good and bad behaviour, depending on whom you ask. And it is he who should be given credit for adding value to the authenticity that the show is known for. After several months on the road doing research in schools, he presented some of the gangster elements that would later become part and parcel of the *Yizo Yizo* legend:

YIZO YIZO: THE POETRY OF DYSFUNCTION

> We started by researching the school situation in Soweto, visiting schools and interviewing kids about their experiences. Bullying, rape, teacher-student affairs and all that. We would then spin anecdotes around the research, write step outlines and then write two or three episodes each at the same time. It wasn't much of a problem for Angus as he spent a lot of time among the rank and file of Soweto. Once, his car was hijacked but he got it back within an hour because of our connections.

Elaborating on the work done behind the scenes, the writer observes:

> The relevance of *Yizo Yizo* was that it was inspired by reality. The characters were based on some members of a feared Mzimhlophe (Orlando West) 'boy bandit' gang who called themselves The Hazels, after a pretty, streetwise girl called Hazel who was every gangster's dream girl. Let me risk coming across as arrogant and say that I was the 'township guy'. I had grown up with the Hazels and other Soweto gangs and had a front-row perspective of their reckless escapades, like raiding schools for girls. I knew how township delinquents thought, felt and lived because I was an interested short story writer for *Staffrider Literary and Art Magazine* for a long time. I provided the anecdotes and the three of us weaved them into screenplays.

After an initial screening of *Yizo Yizo* with musos from Ghetto Ruff, someone described the show as 'the bomb', and thus Laduma Film Factory morphed into The Bomb Productions and later, The Bomb Shelter. That, 'u grand Joe?' line you hear at the end of every episode is actually a line said by Sticks to Thulas in season one of the series.

Even the show's name pays homage to a very specific township dialect which is both unique and generic. The name *Yizo Yizo* means nothing in particular, but it can be reconfigured to mean anything from, 'It's on', 'For sure', to a pre-Wack Jacko version of, 'This is it'. It's all about context, which is something that is at the core of the show. Gibson says:

> We were thinking about names. One morning Teboho said to me that he had heard this phrase 'yizo yizo' in a song and it kind of meant, 'This is it' or, 'This is the real thing'. We never doubted for even one moment that we had found the right title. We also liked the way the words looked and together we fought all the naysayers who tried to persuade us to drop it.

Yizo Yizo gave us some of the most memorable scenes in the history of Mzansi television. Who could forget Bobo seeing a cow after taking some drugs in season two, or Chester handing out exam papers after a teacher forgot them at a bar? Dudu being raped in a chicken den is one of the most harrowing renditions of a crime that has been enacted on the small screen in the history of South African TV and film. Through innovative sequences like this, *Yizo Yizo* de-sanitised the happy-go-lucky imagery that post-1994 South Africans had built about and around themselves.

It went against the grain of the invasive, orchestrated hope that was being churned out by South Africans singing *Shosholoza* in Castle Lager adverts; that single-story narrative that was cultivated in the euphoria of an idealistic, fleeting socio-historical moment. In those heady days, when singing the national anthem at school was still good form, we were a nation numbed by our own optimism.

With the backdrop of that pervasive feel-good era ushering in the ascension of former president Thabo Mbeki to power, *Yizo Yizo* came in from the cold like an unwelcome relative with dirty shoes. The relative who paces restlessly in your living room and starts talking inappropriately about family dirt, uncovering decades-long stains hidden from view, disturbing the false peace and pointing out too loudly that the emperor is, in fact, naked.

YIZO YIZO: THE POETRY OF DYSFUNCTION

Gibson is also not unaware of the trauma some of the actors experienced during the filming of difficult scenes:

> The rape scenes were difficult and quite traumatic for the actors. Scenes of consensual sex were a whole lot easier. We were encouraging a lot of improvisation in all the scenes. The actors really owned their characters. The rape that happened next to the cage of chickens started with an observation of the way in which the chickens attacked their food. There was a kind of aggressive madness to it that was the clue to the scene. Ernest Msibi, who played Chester, took on that madness and the scene took off from there. It was very scary and it took some days for the actors to get over that. The broadcaster usually stood by us, but I do remember negotiating the number of thrusts there could be in the sex scene between Javas and Nomsa in season three.

By unflinchingly depicting people in a township getting on with the everyday business of being themselves without the overarching gaze of whiteness, *Yizo Yizo* showcased that we were and are not as integrated as those Castle adverts had been leading us to believe. To say that *Yizo Yizo* is the greatest TV series of all time would sound hyperbolic to some, but what is certain is that in South Africa, the show provided a much-needed departure from the drib-drab, pedestrian television that had taken over in the 'reconciliation' -fuelled 1990's. It served as a marquee for teaching audiences how entertaining self-reflection could be. A marquee that was later occupied by the likes of *Gazlam*, *Tsha-Tsha*, and, to a lesser extent, *The Lab* and *Home Affairs*. And yet this depiction of what was real could not be done haphazardly, as writer Matshoba explains:

> School rape was an epidemic at the time and the brief had prescribed that we represent reality. The choice was between downplaying the situation or telling it as it was. We chose the

latter. Sometimes shock treatment is the best way to draw attention to serious issues. The biggest challenge was to avoid caricature, or put another way, not to lose the context of reality by creating unbelievable or fake characters. There were some bad characters, like Papa Action, who were repugnant, who we had to write in such a way that the viewers would be compelled to watch because they were an integral part of the story. But the challenge of being careful not to create bad characters who could simply be emulated by young viewers remained always before us. There were many challenges.

It seems to me that often, in critiques of *Yizo Yizo,* the show does not get due credit for its depictions of the complex nature of black male friendships. Consider the bonds between Papa Action and Chester, and how, through the promise of power, they are able to lure Thiza into their circle. The series showcased the reality of how young men, feeling disconnected from their society, often feel the only way they can bond with each other is through violence.

Yizo Yizo was also the launching pad for many of South Africa's now recognised acting talent, some of whom later left the show like an exit wound made by a bullet from Chester's 9 mm chamber. They have since grazed on greener grass. Fana Mokoena on *The Lab* and *State of Violence* comes to mind, before his latest incarnation as an EFF member of parliament. Sthandiwe Kgoroge, in the dual role of the twins Zinzi and Zoleka on *Generations,* as well as a lead role in *90 Plein Street,* is another example.

Contrary to popular belief, however, not all of the show's actors were street bums before making it onto the show. Some of them had actually worked as extras and even in community theatre. But for many of them, including the likes of Tshepo Ngwane who played Thiza, it was through a small agency and the grand lady of South African comedy, Lillian Dube, that they found themselves thrust into the *Yizo Yizo* limelight. Ngwane recalls how he got his big break:

I had just moved from Newcastle to Jozi to come and stay with my dad. I had told him I wanted to do acting but he really didn't believe in that because he worried about how I was going to earn a living. So I ended up studying full time and secretly taking weekend classes and acting workshops whenever I could. I was lucky that Mam' Lillian Dube embraced me. I was just passing by one day and she told me there were these auditions in Rosebank. I immediately caught a taxi and went there and auditioned for the role of Sonnyboy, the taxi driver.

Four days later he got a call-back, and after three call-backs Tshepo didn't get the role of Sonnyboy. Instead, he was cast as one of the leads in the series. With a fade S-curl (which he later shaved off for his role), Ngwane found himself thrust into what undoubtedly became the defining role of his life. But there was one problem; his old man still didn't know he was working as an actor now. A taxi-driving, conservative Zulu man, he had no time for watching TV. 'My dad didn't even see the first episode. He was told by his taxi driver friends that they had seen me on screen, congratulating him on having a son on TV,' Ngwane recalls, laughing. 'I then lied and told him that I was just lucky, that some people had come to school hosting auditions for the show and I got the part. I had to downplay it as much as I could.'

But when the old man saw his son's acting, he accepted the situation and even started taping the show. Who knows, maybe he is the one responsible for all those VCR leaks of *Yizo Yizo* that were on heavy rotation around 2000? For Thembi Seete the journey to getting cast was similar, but having to give up the Boom Shaka 'image' and make room for a vulnerable character like Hazel in season two, was not easy:

I had seen *Yizo Yizo* 1 on what was still called Simunye back then (SABC 1 aka Mzansi fo Sho). I was at a crossroads because Lebo was now doing her own thing and Boom Shaka was not that active anymore. So I spoke to Speedy (from Bongo Maffin) and he introduced me to Mam' Lillian. The first thing I told her was that I wanted to be on *Yizo Yizo*. Auditioning for the show was one of the craziest things I've ever done because I spoke to Teboho before I even went in. I told him to just give me a chance because I was coming from music and this was a new thing for me, and I had to play this tortured character who was surviving rape, so there was a lot of crazy stuff in there all at once.

Innocent Masuku, who played Bobo, says *Yizo Yizo's* success boils down to the fact that Gibson and his team were so willing to take risks with their casting decisions. Most of these risks payed off, but there were some that didn't work out too well (more on that later). Masuku says:

Yizo Yizo is just one of the classics, and it's as simple as that ekasi. And I think part of that goes back to the freedom that we had on set. As actors we were given quite a bit of freedom and we were able to add a lot of input into the script, sometimes even changing the flow of entire scenes, and I think the investment of everybody on that show, during filming, just cut through all the bullshit.

But for Gibson and Matshoba the product of a gritty, gripping TV show did not come without some hairy moments. 'This one time Mavis Khanye gave me a lift to Leeuwkop prison's juvenile section where they were shooting the prison sequence. I got there and some young inmates who were probably from my township started screaming my name. I told Mavis to take me back home,' recalls Matshoba. Gibson relates some hair-raising moments:

Ronnie Nyakale virtually strangled Teboho when he

auditioned for the part of Papa Action. Working with Ronnie was always a lively experience. In this one scene he continually used the word 'motherfucker' or something. We would tell him that he better do it again without 'motherfucker', and then he would get back into character and do the scene again – and he would say 'motherfucker' again. This happened many times over. He couldn't do the scene without saying, 'motherfucker'. Eventually we just had to fix it in the edit. The bash at the end of episode five in season one, when things fall apart after the departure of the principal, felt as wild during filming as it looked on screen. The crew were at the end of their tether and at the end of that night, I felt like I had been through a war.

And it wasn't just on set that things began to go awry. There was a widespread public outcry and calls to can the show after parents started complaining that the series was corrupting their kids (if only they could see the kind of things that they post on their Tumblr accounts now, they would never stop throwing up). At one point the former Minister of Arts and Culture, Lulu Xingwana, called for the show to be taken off the airwaves, during a sitting of the House of Assembly. Imagine that; parliament debating over a TV show. All of this is remembered vividly by Christopher Kubheka, who played Gunman. The public uproar and criticism from public officials created a pressure that eventually took its toll on everyone.

'For me, playing Gunman on the show was a lot easier than being away from set,' he says. He hits a slight pause as if travelling through time to unearth some long forgotten chunks of memory that he left behind, takes a small breath, and continues. 'The reality is that a lot of people didn't understand what we were doing. We were vilified and attacked even while others were praising us. I love what I do, but there were moments where I felt like, "Fuck this, I don't want this acting thing to ruin my life, because of some of the public's reaction".'

The show, whose modest genesis was a wall of ideas in a dingy and obscure basement, was captivating the interest of small screen lovers and TV critics alike. Part of the show's enormity lies in the genius of its creators to get out of the way and let the custodians of the narrative get on with the business of telling a story the best way they saw fit.

The two years between *Yizo Yizo* season one and two were a much needed reprieve for everyone involved in the series. The audiences that had initially been shocked had become somewhat forgetful of the debauchery of the first season. They were beginning to move on, expecting that the likes of Angus and Teboho would come back with more prim and proper stories in tune with the accord of the times. Instead, what transpired was nothing short of a national ambush. The guys at The Bomb could not resist the urge to further pursue the dark themes the first season had grappled with.

A quick survey of some of the letters sent by angry readers to the editors of various national newspapers at the time, complaining about the show, reveals one startling fact. No one, not a single person complained that the story was not authentic. Seeing ourselves for what we are was unsettling. Kubheka aka Gunman remembers this:

> People, and especially South Africans, are ashamed to see the truth, finish and klaar. Everything is just a secret. People want to hide their crap behind closed doors. And now here was this show on TV and suddenly there was nowhere to hide. Now people had to talk about things. They had to start explaining stuff to their kids and a lot of parents and people in general were just bothered by that. Bothered by accountability.

According to Matshoba however, he understood where the public was coming from. He says that there were moments on the show that he was not completely comfortable with, mostly as a result of his own background.

> I was the oldest and probably the most conservative of the

writing team, and there were many instances of disagreement. But in the end some of the stuff I wanted censored ended up on the screen because the directors eventually called the shots. The broadcaster and the Film and Publications Board implicitly approved these things. In a nutshell, I was sometimes embarrassed and thought the criticism was justified.

Matshoba would later exit the show after the first two seasons, and he was not part of the team that plotted the third and final part of *Yizo Yizo*'s rock and roll trilogy.

Another part of *Yizo Yizo*'s jazz is that from the onset, it was a pioneer in documenting the transition from crime in the 1990s, which was heavily influenced by showmanship, to the more blatantly perverse criminal activities of the 2000s and beyond. And all things considered, for a show so widely accused of being violent, it certainly had a shamefully low body count.

But where images of trouble exist, actual trouble often follows. It seems that even though the series is long over, there has been a decade-long pressure imposed by the actors on themselves and from the public at large for their onscreen characters to exist in real life. There have been a lot of *Yizo Yizo* cast members who have been accused of rape, robbery and assault. Art was beginning to mirror life, at least for some of these graduates of what at the time was easily seen as a misfit colony; a breeding ground for the talented and the terminally misguided.

'I was recently in Limpopo and a boy came up to me with a Gunman tattoo and he was still in school, and he tells me that he wants to be like Gunman. That really broke my heart,' says Kubheka, speaking about the shows enduring influence. Gibson attributes this to a lack of audience awareness about the show and its goals, and says that it was a necessary thing to open up the industry a bit more. 'I think that there was courage and openness at the public broadcaster in those years. We opened the door to a more naturalist kind of television and there was a lot of good work done in what felt like a supportive television environment.'

In season three, when the show switched its focus and became more of an inner city story, some of its loyal followers felt hard done by. For two long summers *Yizo Yizo* had been their turf, the one show that documented township reality in a unique way, and now suddenly shades of blackness were being presented in the urban concrete jungle framework. It felt for some loyal fans of the groundbreaking show like a regression; a return to old habits. Gibson defends the decision, saying that it was a necessary part of pushing *Yizo Yizo*'s story forward.

> I wanted the show to move to the city because the characters we had followed were of school-leaving age, and I have always loved Jo'burg city. We were interested in that moment when you are trying to work out what you can do with your life. Everything seems possible and impossible at the same time. We were also concerned about the emergence of xenophobia. I think some of the audience felt that season three betrayed the original formula, which was about a township school.

I'm inclined to agree with Gibson. In fact, season three wasn't a regression, if anything it was provocatively ahead of its time. Tshepo Ngwane, who had graduated from discreet understudy to enforcer-in-chief, was the protagonist to watch. His transformation from charming schoolboy to being the ultimate nightmare of secular mothers around the country (gay) has to be one of the most assured and perfectly executed pieces of character development in the history of Mzansi television. All of those who had been watching him in season one and two, shy and unable to hit on the ladies who had disparagingly called him gay, well, the joke was on them. Before his passing Tshepo confessed that although the role was worth it, it definitely dented his street credibility. 'You get chirped a lot about things like that ekasi. People even now are just not receptive of homosexuality. We tried to open minds but I still feel like that is one of the areas where we failed,' he said.

In addition to its cinematic accomplishment, *Yizo Yizo* would have been nothing without the music. The soundtrack that silhouetted those stark images was an essential part of making sure that the series was situated in the cultural moment, and anyone watching it could directly identify the story as being joined at the hip with the kwaito movement.

The second season of the show provided the emotional blueprint and sonic taste for the next three years. When you look at the roster of musicians who directly benefitted from having their songs on the show, it reads like a who's who of underground hip hop, afro pop and alternative kwaito. Many young South Africans first heard the likes of Simphiwe Dana calling down fire with *Zandisile* on the soundtrack for season three. Or, who could forget the vibrating angst that framed Zola's rude boy lyrics as he talked about bromance, sex, and block parties on the eponymous *Ghetto Fabulous*?

Speaking about the role of music on the show, Matshoba notes that it was about creating a reference that would always be on people's minds. Through the music, the show was able to stay with the audience long after the credits had rolled. Matshoba elaborates:

> Well, music is the foremost expression of social mood and era. Kwaito music was emerging as a breakaway from conventional township sounds like, say mbaqanga or marabi. It was a poetry of dysfunction with neither specific nor profound message, more or less a South African version of Pink Floyd's *We Don't Need No Education*. So it suited our subject very well as it was also contemporary.

Kwaito is often referenced by Americans as a South African version of hip hop. And in many ways (except musical ones), this is true. The kind of influence kwaito had on South African style, language and culture is mirrored by the influence that hip hop had on America from the 1990s and beyond. *Yizo Yizo* rode the wave of that influence in its search for notoriety and immediate visibility. Ghetto Ruff, which was then a thriving indie label, was tasked with compiling the show's soundtrack. They did not just pull the latest chart hit or reinvent formulas from what was then kwaito's ongoing past. Instead they took obscure musicians, like Ndrebele Civilization, and genre custodians like the hip hop outfit Skwatta Kamp, and set them side by side with more established voices like the untouchable Amu, the underrated O'da Meesta and the infamous, self-confessed groupie-turned star Ishmael.

What resulted was a soundtrack that was as fragmented as our national conscious but was effective nonetheless. The show's soundtrack travelled by word of mouth and on radio, and people taped it, sharing it via cassettes. Little known entities like Kyllex and Slovas, although one hit wonders, can today still claim a small green patch in the history of South African music.

Lance Stehr, who is founder of Ghetto Ruff, was one of the masterminds behind selecting and making the tracks for the album. Speaking about this process, he remembers that it was important to include tracks that were relevant to the story.

> We were very fortunate to meet The Bomb team around the time when the first series of *Yizo Yizo* was being shot. They were very interested in meeting around the possibility of doing the soundtrack. At that time Skeem, O'da Meesta, Amu, Kyllex, Ishmael and Ashaan were happening. What was great was that the first single, *Yizo Yizo* ft Kyllex and Mavusana from O'da Meesta, really captured the feel of the show. Before the second series was broadcast we already had the instrumental of *Ghetto Fabulous* done. I had asked the producers to send the full cast down to the studio to see whether there was someone who could maybe rap. Fortunately Zola had been cast as Papa Action, and with his dreads cut off Zola looked the part of the gangster rapper, and he pulled off *Ghetto Fabulous* with aplomb. The rest is SA music history. Lyrically

it set the scene. Musically it had that haunting gangster house sound that was anthemic at the time.

Although the story has been criticised for not giving women a voice, the show's soundtrack was considerably more representative and diverse, giving more female musicians the chance to shine, at times in unlikely spaces. Of all the show's theme tracks, the great Brenda 'Mabrr' Fassie's afro-feminist rendition of *Yizo Yizo* must be the standout joint. At once a cry for help and a call to arms, it is full of enthralling echoes and layered vocals about wanting to make ends meet. Deeply haunting, it was the last kick of a career filled with highs; the crest before the wave hit the shore and started rolling back.

Thembi Seete was one of the contributors to the soundtrack for the second season. The pop diva, known for wearing all black leather, possessing a somewhat husky voice and often relegated to the role of side-kick or understudy to the extremely talented, over the top, late Lebo Mathosa, got her big solo singing break on the show. Her track *Sure Ntombazana*, featuring Wanda Baloyi, was the lead single and a surprising kwaito-tinged call for sisterly unity. Speaking about the genesis of the song, Seete says she remembers feeling frustrated by the lack of sexy female voices in the kwaito genre at the time.

'Kwaito was present but it just wasn't sexy like that. I've always been a team player, and at the time and even now there weren't any female-only collaborations happening. So I decided to do the track and it just struck a chord with not only the women but people in general,' she says. The song was such a hit that is spawned Seete's full solo debut album *Lollipop*, a record that was a joint venture with The Bomb Productions.

And what of *Yizo Yizo* now? Surely a post-democratic South Africa provided plenty of rich narrative for one more season? A kind of tying up of loose ends? Although there is definitely rich subject matter and the necessary distance to reflect on those characters effectively, not everyone seems to agree that we need another *Yizo Yizo*, least of all Gibson. Notwithstanding, there has been talk over the years about a possible season four, but much of it has been urban legend. Gibson is certainly not keen on the idea of going at it one more time, explaining:

> There has always been talk of doing *Yizo Yizo* 4 but I don't want to do another one. I love the series as it exists. I want to do new things. We are doing a show called *Isibaya* at the moment which explores the tensions between traditional and contemporary values in South Africa. I am also developing *Hotel Kalifornia* – a near future Johannesburg love story-cum gladiator narrative, which confronts the growing disparity between the privileged and the underclass in our world. I feel lucky to have grown up in a society where I have been able to witness such dramatic change. History unfolding at high speed. South Africa, in its ugly beautiful way, is always interesting. Often wondrous and often heartbreaking.

Although it seems almost certain that, barring a scramble for ratings by the SABC, we will never see another season of *Yizo Yizo*, the show and its legacy (that dirty word) is still without equal. *Yizo Yizo* was meant to be cathartic; an exorcism of social demons via the medium of television. Instead, through its irreverent upfront narrative, Yizo Yizo captured the early labour pains that come with freedom. It was not just a TV series, it was a symptom. An early smoke signal. Watching the program with the benefit of hindsight, you are able to pinpoint exactly where we begun our descent.

XI

THE GANGSTA MOVIE
Esinako Ndabeni

Tsotsi (2005)

'DECENCY, TSOTSI. WA E TSEBA?' *(Decency, Tsotsi. Do you know what it is?)*

This is a fair question to ask someone who has just stabbed another man on a train without breaking eye contact as he watched the life leave his victim's eyes. The most interesting thing about the movie *Tsotsi* is that, right off the bat, we are forced to deal with the fully-grown tsotsi figure. There is no building of empathy to cushion us and take us through the journey to understanding Tsotsi's (so brilliantly played by Presley Chweneyagae) dastardly act. Instead, we are immediately faced with a young man who, quite indecently, repeatedly stabs a man in a train and calmly holds him up while the commuters get out so that nobody can see. There is no harrowing childhood, no background to this tsotsi's lack of basic human decency.

After the bloodcurdling moment on the train, Boston, one of

the robbers, is puking and cannot quite come to terms with his friend's ruthlessness, so to speak. He is almost taunting Tsotsi as he asks him whether he knows what decency is, what his real name is, where his father is. These questions then trigger a flashback to Tsotsi's terrible childhood, where he ran away from his dying mother and abusive alcoholic father to live on the streets and sleep in underground drainage pipes. Of course, Tsotsi then beats the living shit out of Boston.

Early on in the film, right before he gets into the complicated mess with the infant child, we see Tsotsi crouching under a tree in the suburbs as he waits for someone to either come out or go in so he can break into the property. This guy 'ngumdlwembe nyani', man. The first song of the film, Zola 7's *Mdlwembe* seems to have been written specifically for this character. Zola 7 once explained the term 'mdlwembe' to Aryan Kaganof in his documentary *Sharp Sharp!* in the following words:

> 'Mdlwembe' means 'stray dog', a dog with no owner, right. A dog with no owner will eat from a garbage can, bite when it has to, run away when it has to. It's got rabies and it will basically mess up your lawn if it feels it wants to use it as a toilet, right? Unfortunately, in life there are people who behave themselves exactly like that. They are always a thorn in society, they are always bugging people, they're always trying to hijack a car, trying to take a bag from an old lady and these people, we refer to them as 'imidlwembe'. Basically the song was dedicated to them so as to say, 'The good people are taking back the streets, we are taking back our pride. We're taking back the reason why we fought for this country to be liberated. We will not be bugged by a young kid just because he's packing a gun. We're not afraid of them anymore. So, it was a warning to the minority of criminals that this country is better than that. And because people related to that and they were sick of what was happening, it blew up and became a big song.

THE GANGSTA MOVIE

I grew up in a town called Mthatha in the Eastern Cape. When community members saw a tsotsi trying to rob someone, I would hear a loud 'Hayi!' and then they would all gather around and beat him within an inch of his life. My mother says that back when she was pregnant with me, she was a part of an anti-crime activist group in Mthatha. I have never liked mob justice. I have always, perhaps quite naively, believed in the rehabilitation of even the worst of crooks. But people in town would put all of their energy and frustrations into beating up the mdlwembe of the day. Perhaps it was out of sheer exhaustion from the terror that they felt in their everyday lives, frantic from the fact that this could happen to them at any time. I always ran to watch and stared in shock and horror as mobs yelled and went on to beat the tsotsi to a pulp. It scared my young mind.

Tsotsi has two versions: the leaked, contraband version and the final, official cut which I suppose was changed to maintain an element of surprise after the leak. In the leaked version, the ending is that Tsotsi is gunned down as he attempts to take a bottle with the baby's milk out of his pocket. The version I watched to write this chapter, however, ends differently. And, as I was watching, I had not yet realised that Tsotsi had two different copies with alternate endings. I vaguely recalled him getting shot and my heart started to beat really fast as he handed the baby back to John Dube (played by the iconic Rapulana Seiphemo). Even though I had watched with disgust as this young man stabbed a man to death, antagonised a man who could not walk, beat his own friend within an inch of his life, shot one of his friends... I still could not bear to watch him get shot.

I have been robbed on my way to school before. A man persisted in asking me for 50 cents and when I kept saying, 'No, sorry', he reached out in an attempt to stab me as I had my phone in my hands. I screamed and threw my phone on the floor. 'Take it!' I yelled. Luckily, I was unharmed. But the experience was traumatic enough to give me anxiety each time a male figure approaches me. Because I'm stubborn, I continued walking to school (but I was crying so hard that one of my tutors sent me home). So, I know the terror that tsotsis instill in people. But I still struggle to be okay with the fact that Tsotsi had to be gunned down.

'Tsotsi never went to school. He doesn't understand decency.' This statement, this idea that Tsotsi doesn't understand decency because he never went to school, unsettles me. Not only because it suggests that decency is a trait that can only exist in learned people but because, as one reflects, the flashbacks to Tsotsi's life eventually create an understanding of the kind of life he lived and how it influenced the kind of person he became. Of course, this is an argument I will never win, nor be totally convinced of my stance. It's the never-ending argument of the battle between personal agency and structural socialisation. One can never really account for how two people raised in the same way end up on completely different paths.

When is it one's will to become a bad person, and when is it systems that have created the monster? How does one begin to tell a young man who grew up on the streets that he is responsible for the trajectory of his life? That his indecency is a result of something broken inside of him? Perhaps Tsotsi really does not know the meaning of 'decency' because he never went to school. After all, as Zola 7 explained, umdlwembe will bite anything when it has to.

Still, there is an element of self-awareness to Tsotsi's character. He reflects this when, as he tires of the crying, he takes the baby to the same joint he used to sleep in, with the intention of leaving the infant there. When he gets there, a young boy tells him to 'fokof' and I can't help but realise the loss of innocence that accompanies trauma. Tsotsi seems to realise this as well, as he changes his mind and chooses not to dump the baby there. It seems to me possible that he doesn't want to be responsible for changing the baby's trajectory. He may not fully admit it to himself, but he wants to ensure that the baby does not end up becoming the kind of person that he has become.

In this way, I get a sense of the lack of agency that Tsotsi has had in his life situation when it becomes clear that this is not a life that he would want to consign another's childhood to. Of course, one can always argue that Tsotsi's indecency is in putting himself in the position where he winds up with the helpless child of one of his victims, a situation occasioned by his criminal acquisition of said victim's car. However, I see his decency in that moment. And that's the thing about so many criminals. It is that once you see the full picture, know the whole story, you cannot bring yourself to hate them. They are our uncles, people we used to play childhood games with. People who have shown 'decency' at one point or another.

This becomes even clearer when Tsotsi encourages his friend, Boston, who seems very enthusiastic about formal schooling, to go and write his matric examinations. These small things communicate an innate desire to escape his own overpowering circumstances. He makes the promise to 'phanda' (hustle) for Boston to be able to afford another chance at education. Of course, there are no prizes for guessing what his 'hustle' is going to look like.

To add to Deumert, who says that the 'tsotsi' is also an almost mythological figure representing aspiration, Tsotsi in the movie is cast as a human being with personal experiences that make up the man. To me, Tsotsi's character doesn't seem to be simply that of the rebellious black man who has decided to work outside of the establishment and has no patience for professional blacks, whom he views as servants of the white man. He is not the Lucky Kunene of *Jerusalema*, for example, who decides to embark on a path of 'affirmative repossession' as he hijacks entire buildings from the white establishment. Instead, Tsotsi comes across as a reckless, trigger-happy, traumatised and desperate young man. There is very little calculation in his criminal activities.

The very first introduction to the kind of life he has lived is the flashback to him as a little boy, running frantically with tears streaming down his cheeks. I'm not trying to argue, of course, that there are no criminals and gangsters who actively and methodically choose the path of criminal enterprise, going the way of the outlaw. However, the way that Tsotsi's story unfolds is that it is essentially hopeless from the get-go; he is largely a victim of circumstances. And, in the barenness of his little shack, we know that his criminal activity is a hand-to-mouth occupation. He leaves little to be admired.

In contrast, the character who seems to have intentionally rebelled is Fela (played by Zola 7). Fela appears only fleetingly in the film. However, his character fits the image of the aspirational township gangster. In a scene at a tavern, Boston asks Fela whether he can spell decency. He can. When he is asked what it means, Fela quips that, 'Decency means making a fucking decent living, sonny'. *Decency means making a fucking decent living sonny*. Fela has clearly given this enough thought to make clever retorts and to rationalise his choices to himself. There is evidence here of very calculated choices being made. For me personally, it's hard to think about crime without hearing my father's voice in my ear once again, telling me about how unfortunate his upbringing was and how he has never used that as an excuse to engage in dangerous criminal activity.

Furthermore, it's almost impossible for me to have this conversation with myself without thinking about the backlash that might result from giving off the impression that I'm sympathetic towards criminals and/or supportive of crime. However, there is something incredibly indecent about poverty. We live in a country where morality and criminality are conflated and made a zero-sum game that does not consider the structural systems that lead to certain behaviours. I believe that the movie *Tsotsi* problematises and interrogates the complexities of this discussion quite powerfully.

Mapantsula (1987)

'What do you call a kaffir with an AK 47?'
'Sir.'

The thing about black people and respect is that it is something that we have to spend our lives fighting to earn. We do not have the privilege of being born worthy of respect. We have to be exceptional or, at least, as the character Stander says in the movie *Mapantsula*, we need to be carrying a big gun. I'm kidding of course. Don't go out and get yourself a gun. But you get what I mean. The definition of a tsotsi in the Oxford Online Dictionary is 'a young, black, urban criminal'. This definition caught the attention of 'Black Twitter' in January 2017. People were upset at what they felt was criminal activity being racialised when it is not an exclusively black thing. Well, sure, criminal activity isn't confined to black people. But the word 'tsotsi' is. I say this because there is a politic of refusal to the conduct of the tsotsi figure; a rejection of whiteness.

The translation of the word 'lova' as given to Panic by his girlfriend, Pat, in this iconic 1987 movie is 'loafer'. Literally, a person who does not wake up and go to work like other upstanding citizens. Indeed, as the movie progresses, Panic makes it clear that he has no interest in taking the same public transport every day to go and do underpaid labour for white people. It becomes clear to me that this particular tsotsi figure is rejecting certain establishment ideas about productivity. Capitalism truly is a scam that we have been cornered into, in the black experience. The concept of paid labour, of the work ethic, has been racist from the moment Jan van Riebeeck landed on the Cape's shores.

Structural barriers to the (capitalist) success of the black person were put in place precisely for the black person to be forced to provide his labour cheaply, while being called lazy and therefore undeserving of dignified compensation. I believe that this is what 'ulova' Panic was responding to. I say this with the hopes that I have illustrated the limitations of thinking of the tsotsi figure as a radical attempt at fighting whiteness and its notions of subversion and hard work. I hope that it is clear I have no intention of romanticising the experience of the urban black criminal, for he almost never has a positive life trajectory and usually does a lot of harm to other black people.

While these gangster films differ, it is also clear that there is a context that these characters; Tsotsi in *Tsotsi*, Panic in *Mapantsula* and Lucky Kunene in *Jerusalema* are responding to.

Mapantsula was South Africa's first tsotsi movie. Set in Johannesburg and Oliver Schmitz and Thomas Mogotlane, the film tells the story of Panic (played by Thomas Mogotlane), a disillusioned bus driver turned small-time tsotsi who rejects the idea of working for the white man.

He has come to the conclusion that black people dedicate their lives to slaving away and only earn peanuts. Subsequently, Panic gets caught up in a life of crime. His modus operandi is to target white people roaming the streets of Johannesburg and rob them. Panic is the cocky, fearless criminal who is unafraid to stick his knife out to threaten his victim for the day if any attempt at protest or flight is made.

That is, until he is arrested at a political demonstration. Because his politics are not the mainstream resistance, anti-apartheid politics, he isn't even actively protesting at this demonstration when he gets arrested. He's just looking for someone. When he is imprisoned, interrogator Stander demands that Panic sign a document confessing that he and Duma, a trade unionist who is leading the fight against apartheid, were working together in so-called terrorist activity. The story is told in somewhat messy flashbacks that require concentration to follow, and the attempt at mystery is exhausting.

However, the film is important as a first of its kind in South African cinema. Its significance as a historical document cannot be doubted. While Mapantsula is a gangster film, it is also a very loaded commentary against the apartheid regime. The lens is focused too much on the brutality of the apartheid police to convince me that this is a story that is just about a tsotsi called Panic. In the same vein, this shouldn't be surprising because the tsotsi figure did emerge from the society created by apartheid, and the story of apartheid and the story of Panic the pantsula cannot necessarily be separated.

What strikes me most about the film, taking place as it

does against the backdrop of anti-apartheid resistance, is the juxtaposing of the tsotsi figure and the so-called black radicals. In their rejection of the apartheid system, the black radicals decide to form a collective struggle to attempt to change things. In contrast, Panic's rejection of the system leads him to a life which, while it is still in a sense one of protest, serves him and him alone.

We see this clearly in the scene where prison guards bring food to the cell Panic is sharing with political prisoners. The prisoners refuse to eat the food, demanding a collective dignity, but Panic digs right in because he is hungry. This scene prepares the ground for Panic to, quite believably and expectedly, collaborate with the devious police plan to implicate Duma and secure trumped up charges against him.

After all, Panic is not interested in politics, right? Besides, by this point in the story we have already seen Panic squealing on a fellow crook before to get himself parole. Why would he not do Duma dirty, who he dislikes anyway because his girlfriend has a crush on the activist? Panic has not shown any of the redeeming qualities that the tsotsi figure is often imbued with in tsotsi films. Instead, he routinely tramples on those he can exert his limited power on (outside of prison), and fears those whom he does not have power over (inside). And yet, in a surprising move, Panic refuses to sign the papers that Stander wants him to sign, incriminating the political renegade Duma, and ultimately makes space in his personal activism for a collective activism. This is how he finds his redemption.

Jerusalema (2008)

This movie is my personal favourite of the three I discuss in this chapter. The fact that the English title for the film is *Gangster's Paradise* only makes me favour it even more. *Jerusalema* tells a story of the type of rebellious tsotsi figure that white social scientists so liberally write about. Of course, the film's screenwriter is a white man by the name of Ralph Ziman. Most importantly, though, it tells the story of the disillusionment that would follow after the animated hopes that 1994 brought to South Africa. Lucky (brilliantly played by Jafta Mamabolo) is a young hopeful in the new democracy. He wants to study at the University of the Witwatersrand to which he has been accepted. Only, he has not received a bursary and can't afford the tuition.

Based on a true story, the film begins with Lucky quoting two of his socialist heroes: Al Capone and Karl Marx. 'Al Capone said if you're going to steal, steal big. But Karl Marx said all property is theft.' Today we know that it wasn't actually Marx who originated this phrase, but rather Pierre-Joseph Proudhon.

The terse phrase that 'all property is theft' translates into the idea that we have what we have because someone else does not have it. Of course, when one considers the way that value is measured in society today, it is impossible to completely dispute the statement. Much of what is acquired in the capitalist mode of society is achieved through the devaluing or violation of someone else; blatant theft, worker exploitation, and so on.

In Christianity, Jerusalem is especially significant because it is where Jesus Christ was crucified and resurrected. In this way, Jerusalem has come to symbolise a place of rest. A place of hope. The first song which plays on the soundtrack is *Jerusalema*. Alan Lazar and performed by Sipho Nxumalo, the song portrays Jerusalema as a destination to be desired; a freedom to be protected. Throughout the film, different renditions of the Xhosa hymn *Jerusalema* are sung. Ringo Madlingozi and the late Mandoza sing their own version as well, with Madlingozi's melodic voice singing, 'ndiyakulangazelela, ndakufika kuwe' (how I long for you, I shall come to you).

This hope, this search, this post-apartheid quest is the mood of the film. The new South Africa will be Jerusalema. The irony of a gangster film using the idea of Jerusalem, the holy city, as a theme is not lost on the viewer and is probably intended. At the beginning of his narration of the story, Lucky sets the scene, providing context. 'The beginning,' he says. 'Soweto. 1994. Freedom. The new South Africa. I had dreams.' He talks about the honest living he and his best friend, Zakes (first played by Motlatsi Mahloko and later by Ronnie Nyakale) made, 'selling peanuts for peanuts'. The hopes that he has in this new South Africa, this Jerusalema, begin to bloom when the young Lucky gets accepted to study law at the University of the Witwatersrand (Wits). This is the new South Africa, full of promise.

However, just as soon as he starts celebrating his admission to tertiary study, finishing his last year of school, he is struck by the harsh reality that he has not been granted a bursary, and therefore will not afford to able to afford to study at Wits. Not quite the new South Africa he envisioned now, is it? One day after school, Lucky and Zakes bump into an old guerrilla called Comrade Nazareth, who received military training in Moscow in the days of exile and the armed struggle. As they chat, Zakes reveals that Nazareth is involved in car hijacking, to which Nazareth responds with the words, 'It's called affirmative repossession.' Shortly after that, Lucky and Zakes commit their first robbery in an attempt to get tuition money.

After that, they swiftly become entangled in a life carjacking. In many ways, this mirrors the story of kwaito. The kwaito generation imagined that the music was a post-apartheid celebration; the soundtrack to the carefree and hopeful times that democracy would usher in. That ever astute teacher, history, has taught us now that the genre died just as unforeseeably as the hopes that peopled the new South Africa.

Ultimately, these gangster films reflect the complexities of criminality in the South African township. Kwaito too was associated with violence, and there were black people who condemned it and would label kwaito artists 'amavuilpop'. The leaning kwaito artists had to a pantsula-style fashion sense, and the inaugural act of naming their genre after an old township gang, also reveals the complexities of the relationship that the black youth emerging out of apartheid had with criminality. Kwaito was associated with violence and seen as a platform for disorderly conduct. Kwaito enthusiasts were characterised as having the propensity to arrive at shows drunk and become unruly. A major and tragic example of this is the late Makhendlas, who shot himself dead after shooting a fan, before he could even perform at his last concert.

The week following the tragic Makhendlas episode, Junior Sokhela of Boom Shaka shot a fan in the leg, further cementing the image of the music as promoting a culture of violent hypermasculinity. Of course, as Thuthu Msomi wrote for *DRUM* in 1998, kwaito pioneers such as Oskido and Arthur Matenga (who managed Brothers of Peace), Thebe and Bongo Maffin contested the idea that this violence was exclusive to kwaito. Oskido pointed out to Msomi that, 'This happens overseas but if it happens at kwaito bashes here there's a huge outcry. Crowd behaviour at kwaito bashes is no different from any type of huge music concert anywhere else.'

Kwaito artists had become notorious for carrying guns, which Arthur Matenga insisted was about personal protection. It is important that we do not pathologise kwaito as purely a 'thuglife' soundtrack. It seems that whenever any black subculture has some unsavoury elements within it, the tendency is to throw the baby out with the bathwater. Violence, no matter where or how it happens, is not the sole preserve of any race or genre or subculture. That is why I believe it was important for Oskido to mention that violence was not unheard of at rock 'n' roll and other music genre concerts.

It is socioeconomic conditions that lead to some social groups potentially being more prone to violence than others. As far as crime is concerned, the correlation between poverty and crime cannot be ignored. And if we agree that the township space was created to give black people economic depression and that this depression leads to crime, then we can all agree that to dismiss the tsotsi figure in his entirety is shortsighted and can only add to the problem.

Of course, engaging with narratives around black people and crime, whether it is done through the white gaze or via black introspection, is a desperate balancing act. I am personally not ready to be dismissive of the idea that the tsotsi's image may be sanitised to gain an empathy which underplays the real harm that criminals do to the black communities in which they live. At the same time, it seems to me that an interrogation of the systemic issues which often underpin the tsotsi's resort to crime cannot reasonably be avoided. It's like walking a tightrope: one fall on either side is fraught with danger for the walker. But that is, after all, our lives. That is the black experience in a single image, hemmed in on all sides by dangers that can too easily be described as self-harm whenever calamity strikes.

XII

Durban kwaito's future, past and present
Sihle Mthembu

I: Future

NOW THAT SHE IS NO LONGER awash with the afterglow of being a newcomer, now that she has disproved the naysayers who said she would not last even a year, now that Babes Wodumo has proved herself as someone who can make songs that rattle speakers across the continent, it's time to talk about the fans that made her. These are mostly women, and by that I mean women of all kinds. Big mommas in their 40s trying to marry the night, teens in crop tops and high-waist jeans with hair dyed blond, purple or red.

The 'Babes Hive' is relentless. They are what makes seeing her live a spectacle. When she arrives at the Artizen Lounge in KwaMashu, north of Durban, for her BET Awards send-off party, groups of female fans swarm around her asking for pictures. Some take videos as she just smiles and soaks in the love. The young girls and their mohawked lovers form a barricade around their queen. They scream out the lyrics to her songs word for word and dance until their faces are salty with sweat. Babes Wodumo is the first female performer, since Brenda Fassie and Lebo Mathosa dropped their mics to join the choir in heaven, to have such a bewitching presence on the South African pop scene.

She has the ability to blend into her own crowd with a chameleon-like ease. Often, when she performs she abandons the stage and with her group of dancers moves to the front of the adoring pack, where she can be at eye level with her fans. She will occasionally pull an admirer from the 'mosh pit' and form a circle for a dance-off, and this is the part of her show that really gets people going. Tonight is no different. As she pops and locks, shaking and twisting as if possessed by a higher spirit, she makes even the best of dancers look like novices. They stop dancing with her and instead watch as she commands her body, improvising like a jazz master long familiar with her instrument.

'Leadership, leadership, we are led!' screams one young woman somewhere in the crowd not too far from when I'm standing with what looks like blonde box braids and a drink in her hands, . By now the moon is out and her latest single *Umngan' wam'* is bleeding from the speakers, engulfing the night. This is a spirit Jamia, a dance of the infidels. The impact she has on her fans is not lost on Babes. 'I love the fact that a lot of them can relate to me because I'm just a girl from the township who loves to dance, and there are a lot of talented young girls out there who look up to me,' she says.

Born Bongekile Simelane, Babes Wodumo's story has been well-documented. We know that she is the daughter of a pastor, that she met her now boss and lover, Mampintsha, (depending on who you ask) at a video shoot and that she has been dancing ever since she was a child. What you might not know is that her road essentials include jeans, shorts, a few pairs of sneakers and caps. Lots of caps. She is also obsessed with the arcade game Cadillacs & Dinosaurs, or Mustapha as it's commonly known, but these days her hectic schedule means that she can't play it as much as she'd like.

Despite having a best-selling album and videos that have been viewed almost 10 million times on YouTube, making her one of the most recognizable faces in Mzansi music, the most interesting thing about Babes is how she refuses to lean into her fame. She is almost cavalier about her popularity, as if she is aware that this is some kind of con. 'I've learnt that there are loyal people out there who have been with me through thick and thin. Over and above that not everyone will love you and that's ok,' she says indifferently.

Mampintsha, whose personal and artistic relationship with Babes is something that has catapulted him from being the Beyonce of Big Nuz to something of a low-key mogul, describes Babes as a beautiful soul. 'People are always so shocked when they meet her, at how friendly she is. Because of where South African music comes from they expect her to be this diva, but she will stop and have conversations with people about their lives. To her it's nothing. It's who she is.'

For all her engagements in real life, unlike most celebrities her age (24), Babes hardly engages directly with people on social media. She is guarded during interviews, and between sets at shows you can find her chilling backstage, scrolling through her phone and chatting with friends who knew her before she became a 'national key point'. You could easily underestimate how influential she is, until you see her Original Shandis merchandise sell like hot cakes at the flagship Durban store or realise she's been handpicked by Kendrick Lamar for the *Black Panther* soundtrack. Until you see the actress Jessica Nkosi on *Lip Sync Battle Africa* impersonating the popstress in a lively rendition of *Umngani Wami*, dance moves and all.

Babes Wodumo is the latest star to have emerged from the sound and fury that is gqom, but make no mistake, her roots are in kwaito. With elaborate dance moves that are reminiscent of 1990s era pantsulas, which have recently been amplified by an upswing in Durban's drug culture, she is the glue that connects kwaito's past to its uncertain present. The comparisons to Lebo Mathosa are a heavy crown to wear. After all, Lebo was already a star when Babes was still a baby, but one thing for sure is that she's got 'that thaang and girl can swaaaang'.

It's not lost on Babes that now that the wave of her breakout song *Wololo* has hit shore and is starting to roll back, she has a lot of work to do, most of it on herself, but she says she is not even thinking about how to avoid the dreaded sophomore slump right now. 'I have decided to enjoy the success of *Wololo* and make the most of the opportunities that it has presented to me. When the right time comes, my team and I will announce my next career moves,' she says.

The next time I see Babes, it's in a more controlled environment. She is hopping out the back of a mini-bus, signature red hair in tow and wearing all black IVY PARK and a camouflage jacket. She looks a little tired as she walks into the press conference where she will explain that she won't be attending the BET awards because she doesn't have a visa. This despite the several send-off parties organised for her, and the fact that she had been preparing for the trip for weeks.

Only a few days earlier she had been telling me how she was ready to get a taste of life at the top of the pop food chain:

> It feels absolutely great especially because I'm the first lady doing kwaito gqom to be nominated for such a prestigious award. I'm over the moon! I'm a woman, so obviously my hair, nails and everything need to be on point for the event. It's so exciting! I expect a different world all together, and I plan to have as much fun as possible and to really just enjoy every bit of the experience.

Fellow Durban-born nominee and lyrical beast, the hip hop MC we know as Nasty C, went to the US and moved around in the build-up to the ceremony, making his presence felt, doing press runs, video shoots and slaying freestyles on prominent platforms like Sway. In stark contrast, and for reasons that boggle the mind, the queen of gqom's crowning moment on the international stage was being delayed. 'It's not even that I am angry,' she says to a room full of journalists. 'But I am just disappointed.'

It's been a rough few weeks, and this is not the first time that Babes and Mampintsha have been forced to issue a public statement. Following the 2017 South African Music Awards (SAMAs) ceremony there were three main threads that dominated the mass and social media headlines. The first was how happy everybody was to finally see Kwesta shining, the second was how unhappy Zahara was with Somizi's comments about her alleged alcohol addiction, and the third was the furore that resulted from two Instagram videos posted by Babes and Mampintsha about some awards being for sale. This after Babes had left the awards ceremony empty-handed, to the surprise of many who believed that a win was a fait accompli for the Durban starlet.

The videos went viral and sparked a spoof challenge on Twitter, with people impersonating the duo to hilarious effect. The best videos included one from Tsonga hip hop queen Sho Madjozi ranting about not being credited with being hair goals, and another from Khanyi Mbau where she complained about not being given her rightful dues as the original blessee.

'There are quite a few of them that I really loved,' Babes says, taking all the humour in her stride, before quickly adding that she is ready to put the drama behind her and focus on rolling out her single *Umgan Wam*. She is focusing on the future, she says.

> I am currently shooting as many videos for my album as possible. The *Umngan Wam* video was shot two weeks ago, and really it's all thanks to my fans and the gqom music and dance movement that we carry on. The latest video was done at the West Ink Dance School, and at two other spots where my fans were there to celebrate.

Babes and Mampintshas statements about awards being for sale may not have been completely false, but coming fresh in the wake of the awards ceremony they weren't well received because they were seen as coming from a bitter place. The tide could have so easily swung the other way. Babes could have been praised for calling out the corruption in the industry, with pieces being written about her brand of 'black girl magic' and the importance of women publicly affirming what is due to them. But this is not how that story played out.

The music business is fickle and after a year of being adored and praised, people are finally ready to see Babes lose. In the wake of the incident she confesses that the controversy taught her something which is essential to working in the South African music space: timing is everything. 'Everything comes from God,' she says. 'And he shows up in his own time. My dad has taught me to love family and to rely on God for everything.'

What went unnoticed was how, despite the disappointment at the SAMAs, Babes closed off the show with what was easily the performance of the night. Clad in red leather and chains, with her army of backers, she invaded the stage, doing complex footwork, throwing sevens in the air and twirling on her haters. You don't have to be an admirer to know that Babes is easily the hardest working woman in South African show business. You can't coach height.

Now all that's left is for us to let Babes be Babes.

II: Past

It looks like a monument now, with wooden finishes that seem to have suffered the worst of Durban's hot summers, humidity and rain. There are weeds emerging from the crevices of the concrete pathway, and the building hardly seems to earn the name written in black and white on the sign above the door: Billionaire Boys Club.

If you aren't looking out for it you might easily miss it. This is a far cry from the place that used to be known as Afro Fashion Lounge, the venue where Durban kwaito kingmaker DJ Tira cemented his reputation not only as a hitmaker, but as a savvy businessman with his finger on the pulse of every corner of Durban's music scene.

If you squint back hard enough, this is also one of the places that first embraced early incarnations of gqom music and its lifestyle, in a setting outside of the traditional morning bangs of Inanda and KwaMashu. Tira and his managerial posse took the broken beats of the township and helped DJs who played sets there to go legit, making some money whilst surrounded by copious amounts of liquor and women who were seen as up for grabs.

I ask Tira why he had to shut the place down, and he tells me things were getting out of hand. The flowing of libations would last for up to twelve hours and music-hungry fans were dancing holes into the floor. He expounds on the hassles of running the place:

> The cops were knocking on our doors every time there was a party because it would spill out onto the street and people really just never wanted to leave. Yes, it was an amazing time and we did a lot for Durban music and creating the culture of going out, but at some point you have to cut your losses and move on.

Whilst DJs like Tira, Sox, Siyanda and Bongz are rightfully credited with a pioneering role in developing the sound of Durban kwaito, what is equally important is the role of venues in nurturing the sound of the city and giving it a direct pipeline to audiences.

Durban music also changed the very idea of what we understand by a venue. The city's music is tied to the hip with its taxi industry. In the early 2000s, as government cracked down on the city's broken and run-down taxis, imposing laws that compelled drivers to use Quantum taxis as opposed to what was then called Siyaya taxis, a new culture emerged. The culture of 'ukugqoma'. This meant that taxis had to be fitted with elaborate sound kits that sometimes cost as much as the vehicle itself, disco lights, fancy side skirting and even tents.

There were some legendary taxis in Durban. Some of them, you'd have your car parked and when they came around your alarm would go off. 'It was excessive and the kind of thing you'd only see in Durban,' says DJ Siyanda. All of this loud, expensive accessorising of these taxis was done so that kids in matric from the surrounding townships could hire the most pimped out taxi and take it to Durban's beaches over the weekend, over the September school break or any other time they could go on a three-day bender like no other.

They would sleep at the beach and in the taxis, and there would be dance competitions and sound-swinging competitions to see who had the best mix of bass and tweeters. This kind of event was known as 'iExplosion' and it was the spark that set alight Durban's transition from coastal leisure city to 21st century party capital. As DJ Siyanda recalls:

> DJs would use the explosion to hand out their mixes 'cause a lot of the people who came here for the explosion also ran the scene in other parts of the province, so that's how people started building networks that allowed even young amateur DJs to start booking out-of-town gigs simply because they were from Durban.

DJ Sgqcmeza who hosts afternoon drive on Ukhozi FM (one of the biggest stations in the world with seven million listeners), remembers the early days of the Durban kwaito scene. In the early 2000s he was still a jock on Durban Youth Radio and remembers hearing this music that had a fury and a fire to it. 'There was a definite sense of competition but it was good competition; about who could make the best music and which area partied harder. And that's where the best DJs went.'

The Durban music scene and the trajectory of how it has morphed to become a defining part of the larger South African music scene, can be divided into subsections and movements simply by tracing the origins of the venues around it. De La Sol, with its short-lived but energetic bursts of tribal house, is a notable entry. Plush is another, and is a peer to the Afro Fashion Lounge, which was a mecca for deep house fans with an appreciation for a more refined sound. Popular shisanyama (braai) joint KwaMax, for instance, has always had slots on Saturdays and Sundays where new and upcoming DJs can play afternoon sets that can go on for as long as three hours.

It's a crucial development platform, a place where young DJs can cut their teeth and also expose their music to a wide audience, while the audience gets a sample of their style. I ask owner Max Mqadi about the early days of Durban house, and he remembers them fondly. 'What Durban kwaito did was that it gave the young people of Durban a cultural identity that they could hang on to. So when people saw guys like Tira going from being unknown to making it, it gave them a template for success and something to aspire to.'

Places like Skyy Bar, Burn and even Origin not only provided a home for DJs and musicians trying to make a name for themselves, but also established themselves as venues for students and newly employed young, black 'majaivanes' (dance freaks) to transition out of their youth. As well-known and well-connected club promoter Kgolo da Guru points out, many of the places he managed made it a point to attract university students and bring them into the fold. 'University students set the trend and back then universities weren't as closed off as they are now. Outsiders and strangers could come and chill and enjoy a party so that also extended to the club culture. You suddenly had this whole class of young black people who, a generation ago would not have met each other, were now partying together,' he says.

Part of the challenge that Durban kwaito has faced over the last decade is an inability to shake off it's bad boy roots. Many of the artists and networks associated with the music, from venues to radio stations, are connected to a seedy underworld. An underbelly that is defined by drug trafficking, prostitution and car theft. 'Amaginsa (car thieves) have been known to use the music industry to clean (launder) their money but I'd rather not get into that,' Kgolo says, laughing.

This sordid history also finds its way into the music and is a rich source of content. 'If you listen carefully to a lot of the content, that influence, the slang and stories from the underworld, are there. Sometimes they are so subtle that if you don't know who or what they are talking about you might miss it,' says Kgolo.

DJ Siyanda, who found success with his hit *Iwewe*, a song about the joys of sexual favours and not having a 'government tender' or a job but a 'fire vagina' that works for you, is one of the Durban music scene's elder statesmen. As he points out, the sound of Durban kwaito existed before it even had a name. What made it more obscure was that it leaned more on the house side of kwaito's DNA, as opposed to the hip hop influence that defined kwaito from other parts of the country.

> We enjoyed the tempo of house music because dance and movement is in our blood, and to be honest we used to laugh at the hip hop boys and call them 'amaNigga'. That's why the hip hop influence in our kwaito is not as strong. Even now you will notice that a lot of Durban kwaito artists are much more rhythmic in their singing, they don't do bars like a lot of the Joburg artists.

The restlessness of the Durban sound comes largely from the desire to be recognized. The seasons of discontent that come with people perpetually telling you that your city has a great energy, but having nothing to show for it, gives impetus to this drive. In Durban, partying IS labour, it is as much about celebration as it is about escape and self-promotion. DJ Sgqemeza speculates that as much as Durban has dominated the music scene with acts like Big

Nuz, Professor, Zakes Bantwini, Lvovo and the whole Afrotainment stable, the impact would have been much greater had some people not decided to leave for Joburg or, even worse, quit making music entirely. 'So many people who make it big in other parts of the country are originally from here. Can you imagine how many more talented artists don't make it, and what would happen if all of those artists lived and worked here?,' he asks rhetorically.

Here, angst is ordinary. Anger and resentment is a defining part of Durban's musical aesthetic. Nowhere is this more apparent than in DJ Bongz's 2007 release *Sthandwa Sam*, an album that marks a point of return for despondency. The 13-track record, a holy grail of Durban darkness, is a postscript for a departed lover. Speaking about the album, he tells me that it is only natural to make such a pithy, reflective, soul-and-bones-baring memoir when music is your only outlet. 'When a relationship ends you need something to help you heal. For me I turned to music, and it was only later that I realized that all the songs I'd made were about her.'

Besides the staccato grooves of *Stuck On You*, or the desperate poetics of *Sthandwa Sam* and *Sobuya Sibonane*, one of the standout tracks on the album is *amaSavannah*, a track about inspiration, the loss of it, and how it can be revived with an ice cold six pack of the potent cider in studio. As Bongz points out, he depended a lot on searching out the bottom of many a bottle during the making of this album. 'It was a dark time and you have to remember that, back then, one probably didn't have the vocabulary for describing these things, but I guess I was depressed.'

Pilastos, track seven on the album, is the real gem on this record, however. In six minutes it encapsulates everything that enchants and intrigues about this East Coast strain of kwaito. For me, *Pilastos* is easily tied for second greatest Durban kwaito song. (Fisherman's *Happy Song* is number one and *Pilastos* is tied with *Iwewe*, in case you were wondering). *Pilastos* is a great song on its own merits, but it's made even better if you know the Pilastos the song is about. Pilastos is a real-life mythical figure, a club promoter and hypeman but also, allegedly, a drug merchant supplying the kwaito stars of the coastal city.

If Bongz is the godfather of Durban kwaito's angst, Fisherman is the genre's capable young pretender. Nowhere is this more apparent than on his 2010 release *Happy Song*, which features Big Nuz and DJ Tira. This track's title is very oxymoronic, more so in how the song sounds versus how it makes you feel. The elongated bass marries a flaming string accompaniment. It is a restless noise that seems to be coming from a distant corner and yet somehow manages to astonish and allure.

I spot Fisherman standing at a corner at Max's talking to two young boys. The youths are trying to shop him their demos. 'What am I supposed to do with these?,' he asks me after the boys leave. 'It's not like I can help them.' And this is the thing; the veil between stardom and just being a regular guy is very thin in this city. You could have multiple hit songs like Fisherman and be idolised, and yet be a nobody at the same time. I ask him about the anatomy of *Happy Song* and he tells me it was a response to people telling him to make lighter music. 'People want you to make simple sounds that are easy and passive, but that has never been me. And when people push me in one direction I tend to go the opposite way, because at the end of the day I'm an artist and I want to explore.'

The term 'Durban kwaito' was coined by popular musician Zakes Bantwini. Before he became an executive at Sony, before he got married to Nandi Mngoma, before he became known for gyrating on stage to his house grooves with a funky undercut, Zakes Batwini was just another producer. Like many of his peers, he started an independent label knows as Mayoni Productions, and one of the first acts he signed was L'vovo.

L'vovo had made a name for himself as an MC at gigs thrown by DJ Siyanda at Durban University of Technology, where L'vovo was a member of the SRC. L'vovo, though naturally charismatic, was reluctant to take on the label of 'musician'. As he tells it to me, those first recording sessions left him feeling like an impostor trying to fake a new identity.

'I really didn't see what Zakes saw in me, to be honest. But then when the music came out I realised that people loved it, so I had to embrace this role and, what's more, I have to say I loved the attention,' he says. The two recorded L'vovo's debut album *L'vovo Derrango* in Zakes's studio and released *Bayang'sukela* as the first single, a seminal, defining song in the development of Durban kwaito. When Zakes turned the album in to executives at EMI, they asked him what kind of music it was. 'Kwaito, you have to understand, had become something of a cursed word at the time cause a lot of artists who operated under that umbrella were tanking, so when they said, "No, we don't want kwaito," I simply said, "Okay then. It's Durban kwaito"'.

There is this photo of Zakes Bantwini and Black Coffee with an unknown friend in a tiny room. Zakes looked dazed and is sleeping on the floor, whilst Black Coffee sits, balanced on the edge of a single bed. There is African print artwork on the wall and a poster that seems to read, 'The cooking'. When I ask Bantwini about the picture, he simply tells me that it's been a long, hard road and the roots of Durban kwaito run deep.

L'vovo's debut album is the album that catapulted the sound of Durban beyond the city's shores. It married the city's house music with infectious, whimsical lyricism that was catchy and effective. Reflecting on the album, L'vovo tells me he had no idea how big it would be until it sold over 50 000 units and he was performing back-to-back shows in places he'd never even heard of. But the success was not achieved without some hard labour in the studio. L'vovo reflects:

> Most people see us now and think it was easy, but, in fact, for us it was hard because you had to be in studio together, you couldn't do things remotely like now. And then when everything was done, you still had to hope that people would go out and get the CD. Unlike now, when you can access everything from the comfort of your couch. The

infrastructure was very different.

What makes L'vovo's debut project hold up so well is the album cuts. There is no space for any fillers here. In music, lines are constantly being drawn in the sand. The project put the whole industry on notice and served as confirmation that the delirium-inducing sounds music lovers had heard from the DJ duo of Tira and Sox going by the name Durban's Finest, Shana, Tzozo and Professor, weren't just a fluke. The Durban artists were no flash in the pan. Instead, they would become regular fixtures in the local dance music lexicon. 'Once you get that kind of momentum everyone is looking at who is going to come next, and we knew we had some fire and that's why we worked so hard to push it,' says Zakes.

Beezory, who was also a Mayoni artist at the time of L'vovo's debut, also found limited fame and fortune with his hit *Umthethwo Wakho*, about a loose woman who has been swallowed up by the party scene. L'vovo, musing, recalls the exact moment when he knew that something was a bit different. 'We started getting calls from people in Cape Town and remote parts of the country, not just Jo'burg. We knew the music was reaching a different audience then, and sometimes I think we weren't ready for that.'

These days Beezory, just like DJ Siyanda and others, continues to make a solid living as a producer, engineer and touring artist. He travels weekly to places as remote as Newcastle and Port Edward to secure the bag and keep his discography alive. 'It always amazes me how long music can last. Songs can be timeless. You go to places and people remember songs that are ten years old. To them it's not the time that matters, but the memories they associate with the songs,' he tells me.

I ask him what kind of toll these shows take on him and he tells me there was a period where they seemed like too much, but he has learned to adjust. Recently he has linked up with L'vovo again and the two are making music together for the first time in years.

III: Present

You wouldn't peg DJ Tira as the type that would pull off a shiny, orange, two-piece suede tracksuit. But then again you also wouldn't peg him to be ten years deep at the leading edge of Durban kwaito. Torchbearer and son of a jam-in-chief, 'Makoya Bearings' as some in his inner circle call him, is at Eyadini Lounge to celebrate Danger's birthday party.

Nobody I ask seems to be able to tell me just how old Danger is, but then again nobody really cares. Eyadini, which has gained a countrywide reputation for its famous pictures of patrons walking into the venue, which are snapped and posted on Instagram, is packed to the rafters with a decadent mixture of hipsters, party heads and tourists who seem to know more about artisan coffee than Durban poison, the city's famously potent weed.

Among the acts on the bill tonight are Sjava, L'vovo, Zakwe and Big Nuz, who remain a flagship act for DJ Tira's Afrotainment stable. The multi-platinum selling group burst onto the scene in early 2007 with their hit *Uyoy'sholo Wena* and have never looked back. Even then it was clear that Mampintsha would be the star of the group. With his delivery that sounds almost like he is merely ambling along at walking pace, his nonchalance never failed to catch the ear.

Big Nuz are major time-movers in the history of Durban kwaito specifically, and kwaito in general. But before they became that and were plucked out of obscurity, the trio, which then included R Mashesha before his passing, had already been together for half a decade. The band's name references the township of Umlazi from which they come. N, U and Z are the car registration plate initials assigned to cars in this part of the world. As Mampintsha recalls, they had serious troubles making it in the industry, after several false starts and a flopped debut album which came and went at Gallo records. I get a chance to talk to him backstage.

'When we got the deal with Gallo we thought it was the start of big things for us, but it didn't work out that way. We were not given the freedom to be ourselves and the execs wanted to dictate what we did and didn't do, so as a result we kind of just weren't inspired,' he tells me, while fending off the attention of overzealous fans. By now the crowd is in party mode as the MC on stage regales them with regular reminders of who is still left to perform on the night.

After the flop of their debut album, *7*, the three Umlazi boys moved back to Durban, having noticed that artists from the city were finding success in a localised sound. They returned home in pursuit of home ground advantage. A sweaty Danger, moments away from performing at his own birthday party, tells me that this was all God's plan. 'It was very much a perfect storm for us,' he says. 'Because we believed in ourselves. We knew we could make music but the question was, is South Africa ready for us?'

What is closer to the truth, however, is that a higher power cannot take sole credit for the group's exploits. The mastermind, Tira, was heavily involved too, providing leadership and guidance to the band, which saw them leave their peers in the dust. 'They had a lot of ideas but I think sometimes they battled with simplicity. So as a producer in studio you have to steer that ship and sometimes that means guiding the artist against what would normally be their instincts,' he says. With *2nd Round Knockout*, their sophomore album, Big Nuz began a run that ensured they would become a staple act on the local music scene. In two short years, the group went from virtual anonymity to performing at the presidential inauguration. It was surreal. Danger tells me:

> You have to understand that nothing like that had happened in SA music for a long time. Everybody sang along to *Ubala*. It was like whenever they saw us they were possessed. They'd ask us to perform the song everywhere we went. I remember trying to go to the shops and people asking for *Ubala* while I was trying to buy milk.

It's no wonder then that Big Nuz treat the noise around us more as backing music than a distraction. They are used to this. As DJ Sgqemeza points out, the greatest thing that Big Nuz have going for them is their consistency. 'Artists come and go and they too have had their ups and downs, but they've managed to stick together and keep pushing and that is rare.'

Big Nuz have already achieved the kind of musical immortality many early observers like myself had thought would be reserved for Tzozo and Professor. There was a time, a short time, where safe money would have been on them going on a long hit-making run. Tzozo and Professor were the chosen ones, the anointed kings of Durban kwaito, crowned by Oskido's Kalawa Jazzmee stable of greats. Although they remain friends, compared to Big Nuz their joint output has been something of an inexplicable letdown.

Professor and Tzozo's paths and fortunes also could not be more different. Professor books so many gigs that often he has to turn some away, but the same can't be said for his once partner in crime. Since the release of *University of Kalawa Jazmee* in 2010, a stand-alone classic of an album, Professor has cemented his place as one of the most relentless and gothic artists of his generation. *University of Kalawa Jazmee*, with hits like *Imoto, Jezebel, Lento* and *Toyi Toyi*, was not a chant, it was a skanky outburst.

Professor is Durban kwaito's greatest export, a quasi-Christian Zulu whose poetics seemed to smooth out the rougher edges of the Durban sound. Absurd, charming and well-chiselled by Kalawa's legendary assembly line of producers which includes Speedy, Oskido and Spikiri, Professor is very far from being a spent force. But there are more pressing matters at hand than Kalawa's decadent production. The party is going on, but there is a war simmering here too. Over the last two years the relationship between DJ Tira and Mampintsha has become increasingly frosty, and it seems like the end of the trio might come with more of a whimper than a bang.

Mampintsha has accused Tira of wanting to poach the likes of Babes Wodumo and Destruction Boyz, artists who are signed to his West Ink label. The relationship seems headed for an impasse. When I ask Mampintsha what's going on, he laughs and just shrugs. I know to leave it alone. Right now, ain't nobody got time for that. As Danger and Mampintsha take to the stage and unleash their signature tunes, there isn't a still body in site. When *Umlilo* comes on, things threaten to spill over from party to riot.

Watching them on stage, Big Nuz have an infectious command of the crowd. Mampintsha moves, twists and turns whilst spitting out lyrics with an ease that makes you question everything you've been told about men and multi-tasking. Danger, who at one time played second fiddle to his accomplice, is now at his best, shredding on the mic and shedding bucket loads of sweat as he ushers in anthem after anthem. The group know what their role is and they play it well. Theirs is the simple game of creating a few moments of black joy from the curious mess that black life is. But still, I wonder, with tensions between Afrotainment and West Ink rising… Are they ever gonna do it again? For how much longer?

XIII

Mandoza: Postscript for is'gelekeqe es'focused
Sihle Mthembu

I

I HAD WHAT WE CALL IN JOURNALISM 'a full lid'. A plan so rock-solid only a fool could mess it up. I had been assigned to cover the memorial service and funeral of Mandoza by a reputable weekly newspaper *nogal*. Over the course of a week, kwaito legends, family and close friends, backed by legions of mourners and fans would gather at the Ellis Park Arena and the Grace Bible Church in Soweto. There, they would wax lyrical about all the ways in which their fallen hero, Mandoza, had been a standup guy.

I would sit at the edge of the crowd, close enough to see what was happening on stage and on the faces of the stars in attendance, but far enough to not draw any attention to myself every time I went through my phone to check what I was missing in that alternative universe called Twitter. I would take notes on who was wearing what. Mandoza's wife, Mpho, in a black top with floral detailing and a headscarf that seemed to frame her face more than cover her head. Then I'd flash my media card to cumbersome security guards and make my way to the holding areas, where the artists and speakers would sit secluded. I would pester them with a mix of generic and specific questions that would throw them for a loop. Like, when was the last time you actually spoke to Mandoza? Like, what do you imagine is the last song he listened to before he passed?

They would feed me the expected responses; about how Mandoza was a good man; one who had contributed immensely to kwaito music in particular and South African music in general. They would tell me how his death from a brain tumour, on his wife's birthday, had been the most cruel of coincidences, and how he was gone too soon. Later that night, the experiences and interactions still fresh on my mind, I would thread all these moments together into a neat, concise, 1 200 words and press 'send'. Later, the weekly would reward the sweat of my brow. Ka-ching! Paycheck.

Of course, my plan began to go off the rails from the moment I arrived via an Uber that had taken me from Sandton's Gautrain station to Ellis Park at a surge rate of 1.3. The first thing I saw as I got out was a man who looked like he was in his 40s, wearing a blue and white Ellesee t-shirt and brown dickies pants, spilling out of the back of the stadium in tears. He took off his spottie, sat himself on the stairs, and lit up a smoke almost in disbelief. From the distance I was at, I could make out that he was saying, 'Everyone is dead. Everyone is fucking dead.'

I was running late and had missed the start of the ceremony, which was not playing to the 'African time' script and was running on time. Just a few minutes earlier, I had snapped at my Uber driver, who was busy bragging about how he'd been taking people to the venue and making shit loads of money all morning, that at least someone was getting some economic benefit from this tragedy. A few days later an SMS would remind me of just how right I was. MTN was now offering *Nkalakatha* as a caller tune at a rate of 50c per week. The message left me as restless as capitalism itself, but really my discontent had begun with what I'd experienced a few days prior.

But before all that, allow me to take you further back in time. Let me tell you about how the earliest memory I have of actively thinking about death is connected to the bad narration of an old riddle. My childhood friend, Nkosi Zuma, who was also the first person outside of my family that I ever loved, had asked me what came first, the chicken or the egg? Naturally I said the egg, and he told me I was wrong. Then I said the chicken, and he said I was still wrong. He refused to tell me what the answer was. This was before the advent of readily accessible internet, so I couldn't solve the riddle. Instead, for what felt like weeks but was probably only a couple of days, I kept asking my bestie what the riddle meant.

One day, after refusing to tell me the meaning for the umpteenth time, he sighed as though exhausted by my persistent line of questioning, and remarked that ultimately it didn't matter who came first, the egg or the chicken, because death came for them both, and they were both fated to be eaten. What a thing to say, by one young boy to another! I am reminded of this riddle because, when it comes to Mandoza, I'm not sure which came first: the man or the music? I am tempted to say the man, but what does it matter now that death has come for them both?

Back at the memorial gathering, that Mandoza was not a perfect human being seems to be the running theme of the service. In black culture, it is rude to speak ill of the dead at their funerals. This is not the time to 'tell the truth and shame the devil'. Sweeping things under the carpet is not only expected; it's the norm. So, one after the other, Mandoza's musical peers, friends and family step up to tell us what they remember. MC for the day, Kabelo Mabalane, talks about how he and Mandoza were quite a handful back in the day, and how he learned the principle of 'failing forward' from his late friend.

Mandoza's uncle recalls how the family initially found it difficult to accept their son's career in music. When the muso's widow, Mpho, takes the stage, she tells the story of how, even in the throes of illness, Mandoza encouraged his family to make jokes about him. 'When he was sick last year, his complexion went very dark and we called him leather every time he sat on the couch,' she says, and the whole stadium erupts with nervous laughter. As more and more speakers take to the podium, I get the unnerving sense that Mandoza was different things to different people, and that ultimately he remained unknowable to them all.

Later I bump into Magesh, who is wearing a white t-shirt and hat and seems rather underdressed compared to some of the stars in their suits. He tells me how relieved he is that his friend finally got the peace he deserves. 'He was in a lot of pain man, and you don't want to see someone you love go through that. To remember him like that. The worst part is he was worried that... That's all his kids would remember,' says Magesh, before he is pulled aside by an usher telling him to get ready to speak.

Mandoza was no stranger to a rock 'n' roll lifestyle. He had started off with crime before finding the music. He'd done jail time. And even after he found the music or the music found him, he'd been arrested for assault, served stints in rehab and had his car stolen in front of his own house, all the while releasing hits and taking no prisoners. In his later years, however, he seemed to have slowed down.

The last time I had seen Mandoza was at the East Coast Radio Toy Story corporate day. He was part of a group of celebrities that took pledges and helped raise R1.6 million towards helping feed needy kids in KZN. He told me how much the campaign meant to him, because he knew what it was like to go hungry as a child.

Mandoza, the son of Musa Sibanyoni and Nobesuthu Tshabalala, was born in 1978. He was partially raised by his grandmother in Zola, one of the more seedy sections of Soweto. He was named Mduduzi, he who heals wounds, perhaps as an allusion to the difficult relationship his parents had. Musa was a drunk who would go for days on benders. Prone to the disappearing acts of the chronic binge drinker.

It's no wonder then that the defining relationship of Mandoza's adult life was not his love for his wife, Mpho, but instead the relationship he had with his first born son Tokollo, who he'd named after TKZee member Tokollo 'Magesh', also a Tshabalala. Producer Gabi le Roux, the man behind the beats on *Nkalakatha*, tells me he was with Mandoza the day Tokollo was born. He remembers it in detail:

> He had come down to Cape Town to work on some music, and he was just distracted and kept telling me that he wasn't sure what to do and how to be a father to this baby that was on the way. Then the phone rang and it was news that Mpho had given birth to a healthy baby boy. He was ecstatic. We didn't even get to make a song because I had to drive him straight to the airport. He had the window down and was screaming the whole way there. People would recognize him and he'd tell them that he'd just had a baby boy. It was the happiest I had ever seen him.

That baby boy, Tokollo, is a grown man now. I sit up from my seat in the middle rows of the Grace Bible church a few days later when he takes to the stage with two of his younger siblings, Tumelo and Thapelo. Like his father, the boy has a magnetic stage presence and he has the crowd in stitches as he talks about how Mandoza always asked him for fashion advice. But it's his acknowledgement of his stepbrother Thapelo that really gets me. 'I have a stepbrother. His name is Thapelo. Let's not forget him, because he is still alive.'

Thapelo was born in 2003, the son of Mandoza's then 18-year-old girlfriend, Lucy Komotolo. Lucy had fallen pregnant in matric and didn't get to write her exams because she had to give birth. Mandoza's wife, Mpho, was also pregnant at the time, and six weeks before Thapelo was born she had a miscarriage. A tragedy that at the time Mandoza blamed on the media, who he said were making his life a living hell by constantly writing about the two pregnancies. 'I don't want to go through this shit again. My life is already f...ing complicated because of you,' he told a reporter from the City Press. 'You've already caused me so much pain that you're not aware of. I'm 25 and trying to become a man, but you keep messing up my life.'

At the time Tokollo speaks at his dad's memorial service, he is 16. The same age his father was when he got arrested for car theft and was sentenced to 18 months in Johannesburg Central Prison, popularly known as Sun City. Prior to his arrest, Mandoza and his dance group at the time had met Arthur Mafokate, who was a South African music kingmaker. Mafokate had been interested in working with the group, but that window of opportunity snapped shut when Mandoza got locked up. Despite fearing that he might have lost his chance, whilst in prison Mandoza decided to give music another go.

He also resolved not to use the abbreviated version of his name Mdu, because he didn't want to be confused with Mdu Masilela, already a force in kwaito with his monster hit *Mazola*. After his release, Mandoza linked up with three childhood friends: S'bu, Siphiwe aka General and Sizwe. They began making some demos, which they then sent to Mafokate, and called their group Chiskop. But between Abashante, Makhendlas and his own music, Mafokate didn't have the time or resources to take on production for another group. It was here that Gabi le Roux and his partner, Tim White, saw a gap. 'There really was no grand plan,' he says. 'We just liked the energy of this kwaito music and I thought it would be fun to produce a kwaito album with Chiskop. I didn't know that I was forming bonds that would define my whole career.'

From the confines of his cell in Sun City, Mandoza drew a straight line, never losing focus, to the Sun City Superbowl, where a few years later he would scoop several awards, including Song of the Year. He would shake up the dance scene with South Africa's first true post-1994 crossover hit, and ruffle the feathers of the legendary Brenda Fassie who, backstage after the 2001 SAMAs ceremony, snatched a mic from a TV presenter and shouted, 'Fuck you, this is my night. I've won more awards than him,' before trying to snatch Mandoza's Song of the Year statuette from him. The footage of a young-looking Mandoza in a white vest, gold chain and white hat is hilarious, and captures the complexity of fame. One superstar at her nadir, and one just beginning to hit his stride.

On the way home after the funeral, as I think about my last encounter with Mandoza, I wonder if he'd consulted Tokollo about his outfit that night in 2001. That day at the East Coast Radio telethon, Mandoza was wearing a muscular navy shirt and his signature glasses with rectangular frames. Cleaned up, but not over the top. He looked like a pretty regular guy, and if you didn't look twice you wouldn't have noticed that this was THE 'Nkalakatha', or 'Godoba' or 'iSgelekeqe esiFocused' or whatever he wanted to be called that day. You might have noticed that a recurring theme in Mandoza's music is the pursuit of personas; of alternative identities to hide behind.

That day he also looked very tired. 'It's hectic in December because that is when I get the most gigs, so I'm gonna be moving around a lot,' he told me. That was the last time we spoke, and for the life of me I cannot remember how our conversation ended. Perhaps it's better that way. When people we love die we have a tendency to imbue our final encounters with them with meaning/s. Often this happens at the expense of reality, which is too often random and boring anyway.

II

I still have my mother in law's number saved on my phone. She has been dead for almost three years. I don't know why I haven't deleted it. Clearly, I'm not expecting her to call. That would be irrational. What I also know is that initially there wasn't a conscious decision to keep her phone number. When people die there are more practical things to think about. Like who will carry the coffin from the house to the hearse? Which family members must speak at the service, and on which plot of land will the deceased be buried? Should they be close to home so when you drive by you can always remember them? Or should they be far so we can have the space to forget?

Decisions like whether or not to delete their number and what to do with their cellphone come later, and yet they possesses a moral weight that feels unshakable. Everything is so final and once done cannot be undone. Deleting my mother in law's phone number feels like it would be an act of betrayal. She had already been betrayed by her body, which eight years earlier had decided to give her cancer. Deleting her number would feel too much like having to let go of her all over again.

'At death, you break up,' says the poet Phillip Larkin. 'The bits that were you start speeding away from each other for ever.' I wonder when Mandoza the man and the body started to go separate ways. In the year leading up to his death, Mandoza began to have severe headaches, and sometimes his eyes would bleed. After suffering a seizure during a show in Bloemfontein, he had been admitted to Tshepo Themba Private Hospital in Dobsonville where doctors had to revive him using electric shock. This would be the first step on a very difficult, painful battle with cancer. A battle that included radiation sessions for seven weeks and three sessions of chemotherapy. A battle punctuated by severe vomiting and rapid loss of weight. By the time he passed, Mandoza had lost his sight, which is why he was forced to wear those dark shades in his final months.

Illness hurts because it is your own body that attacks you. This cast of blood and flesh rebels to remind you that you are more than your limbs. That in fact the house you inhabit is not your own. Christians call it a temple. Temporary housing. And on September 18 2016, two days before my birthday and on the birthday of the love of his life, his wife, Mpho, Mandoza was evicted from his earthly place of residence. On my better days, I believe that he was moved to a more comfortable residence in the sky, where he is booking shows and performing in another dimension now.

When you have visited trauma rooms and sat waiting in them

as much as I have, you start becoming aware of small things. Like the fact that there are six nebulisers in Addington Hospital's emergency room. There are two functioning sinks, and you could easily fit ten beds in that open space between the medicine cabinets and the seats. You also become aware of how people tend to go. Indian women always seem to feel it the most. They tend to scream and wail, for a good fifteen minutes before finally letting go. Black women on the other hand remain tight-lipped in the face of death, whether they are departing or are seeing someone depart.

Mpho, Mandoza's loving, newly widowed wife, is the stoic in every black woman I have seen in the pale shadow of that unwelcome visitor, death. Her face is hard, and I imagine that in many ways Mandoza's life must have prepared her for this. His absence. What has life with this man been like, Mpho? This star who we also lay claim to, also own, we, the people? The loving legions of fans? Him somewhere out there on stage, churning out his signature tunes with that raspy voice of his, to the delight of audiences whose faces seem to blur and merge into each other, while you at home put the kids to bed. Did you tell them their father was a hot thing? A big thing? Did you tell them that their father belonged to the people out there as well? That he was too 'big' to be hemmed in by the walls of home?

Tokollo is a grown man now. He has seen enough about life to joke in the face of its brutal ending. He is much taller and less muscular than his father, face chiselled and full of youthful purpose. Many of us critics in the arts build our reputations, not on critiquing but on criticising. Or more accurately, complaining. How do you review the memorial service of one of young South Africa's defining voices? It's only later, much later that I questioned the legitimacy of my assignment. When an icon dies their death belongs to nobody, not even their family. Mandoza's death certainly did not belong to some journalist he had bumped into a few times, I was keenly aware of that, but somehow that knowledge didn't negate the fact that his dying felt very personal to me. That

MANDOZA: POSTSCRIPT FOR IS'GELEKEQE ES'FOCUSED

it once again forced me to confront my own mortality in ways I had tried hard to ignore. Mandoza has been gone for over a year now. If nothing else, I am a fan and am still listening to him for words of guidance. Beckoning him from beyond the grave via the medium of his own music. At times he seems very close, as if at my shoulder, whispering words of reassurance. Other times, things are more complicated. These are the dark hours, when I listen to his music and all that is left is a void.

I ask Gabi le Roux to tell me the story again. The one he has probably had to tell more times than he'd like. The one about how, during one of Mandoza's visits to his studio, which was still in his own home in Cape Town, Mandoza had been taking a break from recording when Gabi played a simple melody on the keyboard. 'He came rushing in from outside,' recalls le Roux fondly. 'He looked like he'd seen a ghost. He asked me to play the melody again and I did. His eyes lit up and he told me we had a hit on our hands. We began to work on it and by the end of the day we had done most of what is now known as *Nkalakatha*.'

Mandoza didn't just have 'a hit' on his hands. He had a record that in the first week sold 25 000 units, and would go on to move more than 350 000 in sales. He had a track that would be nominated for the SAMA Song of the Decade and would serve as background music during rugby and cricket games. A crossover anthem, a soundtrack to our hallucinations of unity. It would catapult him from township folklore to the coalface of South Africa's pop mainstream.

As the years went by, *Nkalakatha* would also prove to be an early peak in a career that was filled with many ups and many downs. Mandoza was part of a generation of young black South Africans who, on the back of the promise of democracy, had been led to believe that they could transcend the confines of their colour through their talent, and that such gifts were a magical key to opening other doors. They were a generation who firmly believed that they could use their talents to break barriers, especially economic ones, not only for themselves but for others as well.

Throughout his life, Mandoza entered into and out of various business ventures, to varying degrees of success. These included Tyme, an artist management company which counted acts such as himself, Mapaputsi and Ernie Smith on it's roster, and at some point even a clothing line. Restlessness is the defining trope of Mandoza's life and career. It was this restlessness which, after the best-selling albums *Akusheshi* and *Relax* with the group Chiskop, had forced him out of the comforts of a successful group and into the wilderness of a solo career.

'Uzoyithola kanjani uhleli ekhoneni?' (how will you get ahead by loitering on street corners?) he asked on his debut album *9II5 Zola South*. On this often overlooked and misunderstood debut, Mandoza lays out his statement of intent. This 10-track album actually has only six songs and four remixes (dub remixes were very much in vogue in 1991). Besides *Uzoy'thola Kanjani,* other standout tracks include *Angikhohlwa Langiphuma Khona,* with its sinister instrumentation, and the six minute 21 seconds long magnus opus, *Nizwile Na?*

One of the things that is often forgotten in assessments of Mandoza's musical legacy is his ability to catch flows. On his debut record he showed how deceptively skilled he was at simultaneously spitting his verses and drawing his breath, so that by the time the verse came to an end he'd punctuate it by breathing out. It's a peculiar tool in his arsenal that I have only heard Andre 3 000 use regularly. *9II5 Zola South* was a clearly thought out depiction of the harsher aspects of life in the native township, and was distinguished by the fact that Mandoza chose to interrogate rather than simply endorse some of the popular choices of ghetto youths. The album remains, to my mind, a gem far too little appreciated in his discography.

9II5 Zola South was Mandoza at his most unfiltered and menacing. In the years that followed, he would show flashes of these rough edges, but the attempts would never quite stick. Part of the reason why his star waned over the years was not because he'd lost his talent, nor was it that kwaito was in general on the wane. No, instead it was because he was making music about a life he wasn't living. Having built his name on authenticity, Mandoza had failed to transition the content of his music into the next stage of his life, and increasingly smart audiences couldn't help but notice the disconnect.

You can hear the uncertainty, some might say the false notes, littered all over offerings like *Champion, Ngalabesi* and *Ingwenya*. Mandoza was struggling to embrace his role as kwaito's 'made man', still reverting back at times to that familiar role of the underdog. This, coupled with a slew of artistically misplaced features, combined to create a mid-career many of (even) his diehard fans, including yours truly, would rather forget.

On his influential album *One Day It'll All Make Sense*, Common describes 'GOD' as the process of 'gaining ones definition'. There's no doubt in my mind that Mandoza had a lifelong battle with spirituality. A battle fueled by his inability to find a gap through which he could merge his two personas: that of Mduduzi the man/husband/father/son, and that of Mandoza the kwaito demigod.

It seems like a recurring theme in the deaths of our kwaito stars that they make one last big public appearance before they pass on. In 2008, Abashante's Zombo did an incredible interview on SABC 1's *Live* before dying after a long battle with HIV. Brown Dash had performed in a kwaito medley alongside Trompies and Brickz at the 2012 SAMAs just weeks before succumbing to pneumonia at Chris Hani Baragwanath Hospital. And Mandoza followed in that long line of very memorable and public goodbyes. He was part of a bill of artists that performed during the *Thank You SABC* concert at Orlando Stadium. The event, which was organized by then SABC head, Haludi Motsoeneng, was billed as a 'thank you' gesture to the SABC for regulating that all radio stations at the public broadcaster should institute a 90% quota of local music in their playlists.

At the concert, a frail-looking Mandoza, hiding behind those dark glasses of his, takes to the stage. For a few seconds a hypeman in a red cap seems to be relaying a message to him, perhaps some words of reassurance that he'll get through this. Mandoza takes in the screams of the crowd for a few minutes, before *Nkalakath*a is unleashed from the gigantic stadium speakers. The crowd erupts into frenzy, but Mandoza seems unmoved. Maybe because he has been here before. Perhaps because he knows this is the last time. In a white shirt with 'Mandoza' splashed in gold on the front, he takes the mic and shimmies back and forth, singing along to the backing track of the song.

The most telling moment comes as he transitions from his opening verse to the hook. He is facing away from the crowd and keeps singing. The man in the red cap steps in and nudges him by the arm, turning him back to face the crowd. He never gets a chance to see those jubilant faces and frantic hand signals at his final show. Mandoza's sight had been declining rapidly, and he was completely blind by the time of his passing. By the end of his performance he looks spent, before he thanks the fans for their support and drops the mic.

This is not how we should remember Mandoza. As frail. Sickly. Unable to see. Not fully present. He was one of kwaito's most energetic performers. Mandoza knew intimately the heights of iconography (he was named 77th on a list of 100 great South Africans, ahead of Athol Fugard, Govan Mbeki and Hugh Masekela) as well as the lows of caricature (his collaborations with Danny K come to mind). At his peak, through both his music and his public persona, Mandoza embodied the contradiction of the terror and tenderness of youth.

I remember being in 8th grade and singing *Respect Life* from the *Yizo Yizo* soundtrack, and being haunted by it's quiet desperation. When he said, 'This one goes out to all of my boys!', I felt that shit. The combination of gruff, searing, caring fatherly advice merging into and out of an exquisite, trailing saxophone is nothing short of hair-raising. Mandoza had been preparing us for life without him his whole career. We just hadn't noticed.

Here are some things you might not know about death: John Coltrane and Billie Holiday share a death date. Mandoza and the gospel maestros Lundi Tyamara and Sifiso Ncwane all died aged 38. Here is something else you might already know, and if you don't you will, in due time. Death, though inevitable, is the worst thing in the whole gamut of human experience. Its music sings ominously over our lives no matter how high the notes we hit.

After the memorial service, on the cab ride back to Sandton's Gautrain station, I start thinking about one of my favourite scenes from *The Wire*. The one where Omar, one of the most enchanting and complex black TV characters ever written, gets killed by a little boy in mid-episode, in a corner store, and the show goes on like nothing happened. His death, arguably the most significant in the series, is met with a shrug of indifference.

The scene encapsulates for me the truest thing about death. It is always unexpected. We always believe that it is some kind of metaphor, a teachable moment. That if we are good and we learn whatever lesson it is here to teach, the chasm can be unruptured, the sick can be healed. Things can go back to the way they were. But death is objective and in this way it is one of the few authentic human experiences to which and by which we are all connected.

As we make our way through the world, art tries (but ultimately fails) to prepare us for just how cruel death can be. It is true that people die and we die with them. Time passes, years go by, and soon life blends into death. The message could not be clearer: do not waste your life. The pundits have already declared kwaito dead, but in this moment, on my way to the train station, as the Jozi traffic whizzes by and the city seems to treat Mandoza's death with the indifferent sigh that met Omar's, I have never been more eager to hear the dead speak.

XIV

Producers Paradise: A paean for the men on the boards
Sihle Mthembu

The prestige

AMANZIMTOTI IS A TOURIST TOWN. It's one of those destinations you see on the travel section of the airport bookshop when you are avoiding picking up a guide of Durban's nightlife and bunnychow culture. It's also the place you pass en route to somewhere else. Amanzimtoti is about 20 minutes from Durban. Like its more prominent KZN cousin, it has scenic beaches, a bustling food culture and, on some days (if the waves are not too harsh), you can actually see pods of dolphins making their way up and down the shoreline. It is one of those towns whose social fabric has changed dramatically over the last 10 years, with the rise of development and integration, but its identity remains in the ability to retain a small-town charm.

The story goes that the river 'Amanzimtoti' got its name after King Shaka, passing through in 1826, stopped to have a drink of water and remarked, 'Kanti amanzi amtoti'(Ah, the water is sweet).

PRODUCERS PARADISE: A PAEAN FOR THE MEN ON THE BOARDS

This place is not where you would think to start looking for one of kwaito's most innovative producers. D-rex has been living (or hiding) here, depending on who you ask, for the last seven years. In 2011, at the height of his fame, having won numerous awards and on the back of multi-platinum singles and albums, D-rex packed his bags, closed his studio in Johannesburg, and went cold turkey on the industry that made him. The city was killing him, he tells me.

'As far as the music industry here goes, it's nothing compared to Jo'burg, but that is exactly why I left. I wanted to live a simpler life, and living here is much easier and even more affordable than Sandton, that's for sure,' he says. Something had to change. He tells me:

> I lost my love for producing music. I had started with jingles in advertising, and I gradually started hating it because it was just such a money-driven industry. So then I moved on to music, producing albums, but eventually that also started to feel like an endless money-making scheme. I think at some point I made 300 songs a year, and I just couldn't stomach music anymore. I remember going on holiday and asking my wife to just not play any music. The feeling that I used to get from music had completely disappeared.

Born David Campos, D-rex is the older brother of Justin Campos, the music video director known as Jusgorrilla, whose maverick style of directing music videos has come to define the visual identity of Mzansi music. As a child David grew up listening to music, and by his early teens he knew that music was the path he wanted to follow.

> My dad was a pianist and composer and I grew up in a very musical family. I was playing piano from the age of five, and I used to watch a show on TV called *Di A Rora*. My dad also used to make me record music videos on VHS, so I built up this relationship with a lot of different types of music like jazz, fusion, pop and gospel. I was singing on

jingles and eventually I joined the choir at church. And then, when computers started coming around I was immediately fascinated by them. So that combination of music and computers did it for me. My dad had this studio and it was completely computerised. Eventually at 16 I just decided to drop out of school because I was always in studio and working, and it was all getting too much.

As a young party-lover with a propensity for white powders best ingested via the nose, David was a regular in Jozi's underground house scene of the 1990s. He would hop to and from rave parties in the city for so long that sometimes the days would mutate into each other and the beginning and end of the benders would blur. It was during this period that David got to see kwaito at its genesis. At Joburg's more seedy venues, he was one of the first witnesses to an inventive new way of making music, which included slowing down house beats and spitting repetitive rhymes over them. It was a revelation, and David says he fell in love.

> I was very much part of the early days of house. Back then it used to go by names like acid house, garage house and so on. So when kwaito started and they were slowing down these beats and using rap on them, which I was also a big fan of, I was amazed. Here were the two genres I loved the most and they were being fused into one.

Having witnessed the beginning of the kwaito sound and culture as a fan, and being familiar with both the architecture and the architects of the sound, David wanted to contribute.

> I also felt like the South African music lacked some of that international slickness. I felt like we could take it to the next level. Before I came along, most of the kwaito sound was very repetitive. For me, what I brought into kwaito was to

PRODUCERS PARADISE: A PAEAN FOR THE MEN ON THE BOARDS

move away from this emphasis on having repetitive choruses and instead inserting some verses. Also, the mixing and the mastering wasn't up to international standards, so having worked a lot on jingles I had the advantage of being able to do that.

During his jingle-making days in the ad industry, one of the first musical relationships he formed was with Mavusana, and the two began working on music together. Mavusana had made a name for himself as part of a raw and rugged crew called Oude Meester, and was now looking to shop an experimental new duo with rapper Mizchif, but nobody was biting. The three of them locked each other in David's studio and came out on the other side of that trip with *Summertime*, a groovy, downtempo kwaito record with RnB, house and hip hop influences. D-rex tells me that the idea for the record came from a conversation he and Mavusana were having about summertime anthems.

Around this time, Mavusana also introduced D-rex to Mapaputsi. This unknown would go on to form one of the two defining artistic relationships of D-rex's career. The second would come later, with TKZee's Kabelo, with whom he formed Groove Luv Productions. Soon after he completed recording *Summertime*, D-rex had his first taste of the afflictions of the music industry. The record was released and D-rex never made a cent from it. 'We got a lot of airplay with that but eventually our deal with Lance and Ghetto Ruff fell through because Mavusana had gone and secretly signed a deal with Mdu. So it was this big fight. That was my first radio hit but I never made any money from it.'

The video for *Summertime* features Mizchif and Mavusana engaged in some poolside fun, beach balls and squirt guns in hand. But the heartbreak of not seeing a cent from his first hit single was something that stayed with D-rex for years to come. A producer's place is in the music. The producer has traditionally never had a clear position in the history of kwaito, because the artists have always been seen as the drivers of the music and the narratives we attach to them. But the cold hard fact is that often the real artist was the producer. Many kwaito musicians could not play an instrument or program a beat. This latter fact also explains why, for many of the kwaito 'artists', when the sound died they died along with it; because reinvention is impossible when you don't know how to use the tools you need to survive.

Historically, kwaito producers have also been sidelined simply because of the realities of the music industry. The constant meddling of labels and record companies in the creative process, in deciding collaborations and in picking singles, means that a lot of the hitmakers who made their name in a more free-form music business are now forced to operate in a very different environment. An environment where creative control is non-existent, and, often, neither is the money. They are also forced to 'compete' with legions of other young producers working out of their bedroom studios, who are willing to work for less and put up their music for free online. As Guffy points out, it's a hard pill to swallow.

> You build up this whole catalogue, and a huge part of that is you building up your reputation; your value and worth as a producer. And then you now have to compete with these young producers who don't really know the music business, and so are willing to do anything to work with certain artists. It makes it difficult for one to compete in that kind of environment.

Long-term collaborative partnerships are one of the ways in which kwaito producers have been able to define their sound. Think of DJ Cleo and Bricks, or D-rex and Mapaputsi, or Gabi le Roux and Mandoza. The familiarity and instinctive understanding that results allowed for artists to produce a consistent body of work. Unfortunately these kinds of long-term partnerships are no longer commonplace. The reality now is that artists will parachute

PRODUCERS PARADISE: A PAEAN FOR THE MEN ON THE BOARDS

the hot producer of the moment in, get a beat from them and voila! A hit can be manufactured without the artist and producer having ever met each other. D-rex recalls a different time:

> I didn't go the same route as a DJ Cleo, for example, who would always be out at events trying to meet people and build networks. At some point I just locked myself in studio and people would always be bringing other people. That's how I met people like Khabzela and Mavusana and Mapaputsi, and then we'd just start working together. After *Izinja* with Mapaputsi sold over 100 000 units, a lot of people started to trust whatever direction I wanted to give them. I think I also started to get a bit of a reputation for the way I worked in studio, because I didn't allow guys to drink. I also used to push hard for the vision of the song; I believed a lot in strategising around what the song is about and what it should sound like.

In the course of my research it strikes me that one of the other challenges of being a producer is that people don't seem to know what it is that you do. I speak with Jamela, who worked for Arthur Mafokate and 999 for 10 years and helped make possible some of his hits like *Sika Lekhekhe*. Jamela tells me that, for instance, people think that Arthur programs beats, which is not always the case:

> He might do the beats on some songs, but not always. On others he might just give you a vision of what the song must be like sonically. In that case he would provide vocal and arrangement direction, and be responsible for getting the artists into the studio. He is not always on the boards, so what he does then is different, but it's still producing and it's still important.

But here's the thing: the value or the role of the producer is easy to underestimate. I say this because the more you hear and learn about kwaito music, the more one thing becomes glaringly clear: a lot of this stuff was completely random; it was never deliberate or part of an elaborate plan. So how can you give credit to people for choices that were never conscious to begin with? I ask D-rex this and he attempts to answer the question with some honesty:

> I think sometimes we get caught up in whether some of the choices producers make are deliberate or not. For me, what is more important is for us to understand that, okay, as part of the creative process you might start somewhere but end up in a completely different place, and it's only right that producers get credited for being part of that journey, and not be systematically written out of the history of the music.

I ask D-rex if the fear of being written out of the history of kwaito is part of why he decided to change his name from David. It was not uncommon to hear his moniker, 'D-rex', being shouted out by artists on singles he had worked on, which is testament to the relationships he was able to build with them. As to the name, he tells me it was a necessary evil after years of being blackballed by label bigwigs and radio stations.

> Because I was a white guy trying to get into kwaito, people were always trying to block me, from station managers to compilers. Iggy Smalls tried to block me. I remember him telling my friends that Gabi Le Roux had got into kwaito and now I was doing it too. Things like that made me uncomfortable, like I was being limited. This was the music I loved and it came naturally to me. So I changed my name to D-rex and everybody thought I was black, and by the time they'd realise that I wasn't, it was too late. I was already one of the biggest producers in the country.

We regard kwaito as black music, but what then do we say about the fact that the biggest hit in the genre, *Nkalakatha,* was produced by a white guy (Gabi le Roux)? What do we say about the fact that, despite having removed himself from the hotbed of the industry for longer than a decade now, some of D-rex's best music holds up better than singles released two weeks ago, with twice the amount of resources that he had?

Another major point of contention in kwaito music is the art of sampling. Many of the most important songs in the history of the genre are rooted in a sample, sometimes deliberate (like TKZee's use of *The Final Countdown* on *Shibobo* and even a re-recorded excerpt from Joni Mitchell's *Big Yellow Taxi* on *Phalafala,* or it could be completely accidental, like the way Mgarimbe appropriated Aaliyah's *Rock The Boat* because it was one of the few available presets on Fruity Loops.

Gabi le Roux hates samples. 'It feels to me like an easy tactic. Like taking a known song and using the best parts of it for your own song. I like to create new things. Kwaito is challenging music and that is why I always steered clear of samples, because I always wanted to try and create something new.' D-rex, however, has a more laid-back approach as far as sampling is concerned. 'At the time, sampling was not just a kwaito thing. It was a global trend. It was our expression of what was happening around the world. I think there is a place for sampling and I don't see any problems with it,' he says.

D-rex views music as both a calling and a mechanical process. As something useful to pass the time, but also a practical undertaking. He is surprisingly Zen about the whole thing. Perhaps this is because he is now a born-again Christian and being a zealot for kwaito music isn't high on his agenda. These days, he is focused on spending time with his wife and kids, and running an online school where he teaches people from around the world how to make music.

This is definitely not the same man who, at the height of his foray into kwaito, made dozens of chart-toppers. But this is not the first time I see this almost complete turn from the D-rex generation. To have come of age in Mbeki's South Africa means you were always in danger of being stripped bare of all innocence, and D-rex is no different.

The pledge

The history of kwaito is a contested space. What is clear is that African musical and oral strains and hip hop and house converged to create a baby. A baby whose roots run deep and disparate. They could be traced back to the successes of afro-bubblegum in the '80s by way of Brenda Fassie and Chicco Twala. You can also hear strains of it as early as 1987 in Senyaka's *Fuquza Dance* and *Go Away*. These were the precursors of kwaito, featuring a chopped up and slowed down beat, accompanied by repetitive, rhythmic rhyming.

Kwaito's roots remain elusive because, in the pursuit of accuracy, musical historians seek a finite commencement date for the genre. Some have even named the day Arthur Mafokate released *Kaffir* as the day the earth stood still and the song and album drew a line in the sand to mark before and after the birth of kwaito. But kwaito is infinite and has many founding mothers and fathers, who often contributed inadvertently to the formation of this special music.

The likes of Monwa and Sun, JE Movement, New Age Kids and 2 Black 2 Strong, through a sound which emphasized black township musical expression, whimsical anthemic undercurrents and funky twists, are important strands in the DNA of kwaito music. Spikiri is not shy to say that it was Chicco who ignited his passion for music:

> I was inspired by Chicco. I used to watch him working and composing songs for Brenda Fassie, and I would think, 'I want to be just like him'. We used to be dancers in the township and we were always winning competitions. So there was this guy called Steve who used to be a tavern owner and knew Chicco, who happened to be looking for dancers.

PRODUCERS PARADISE: A PAEAN FOR THE MEN ON THE BOARDS

> We auditioned successfully and that's how we got to be on the *I Need Some Money* video.

Spikiri may have got his first big break when he auditioned and got a job as a backup dancer for Chicco. He later graduated to playing the keyboard, but his love for dance never left him. And it would make its way back to him later as a member of Trompies, where he would choreograph and coordinate dance tracks for the quartet. 'Kwaito is our culture. That's how me and Jairus grew up. We were dancers. But it was bigger than that. How you dress, the language, how you talk. It's a culture, kwaito. It's a manual about how we survive in the ghetto,' he says.

Bubblegum music played an important role in creating the climate that allowed kwaito music to turn into a storm in the 1990s. It gave future artists of kwaito a home before kwaito became a thing, before it even had a name. One such example was Cool Spot Productions, founded by Mally Watson and Ken Haycock, which released benchmark records in the archive of black South African pop such as those of Monwa, Xilembe as well as Steve Kekana. The label also released a small album in 1989 titled *Where Were You?* by a then unknown duo called MM Deluxe. This was Mdu Masilela and Mandla Spikiri, who had become friends through both being part of the bubblegum music scene. They had now formed a musical bond that stretched beyond the limitations of sweating in the background as dancers whilst their idols unlocked the jams. Spikiri recalls how MM Deluxe came to be:

> Mdu used to play keyboard for CJB and at the time I was also playing keyboard for Chicco's band. We were the only young guys in those bands because everyone else was a grootman (older than us). So we would chill together quite a lot, because we couldn't hang out with the older guys, and that's when and how we decided to form our own group.

Due to low production budgets, session musicians and backup dancers often had to dabble in production and arrangement during studio sessions. This is the beautiful accident behind the formation of MM Deluxe. Whilst Mdu and Spikiri were messing around in studio, they began using time leftover from other artists' recording sessions to start making their own songs. They didn't use all live instruments of course, and some of what you hear on MM Deluxe are purely digitised sounds. This was the beginning of something new; a harbinger of the insistent programming that would come to define the sound of kwaito through the 1990s and beyond.

A case can be made for regarding *Where Were You?* as the bridge that connects the over-produced instrumentation of 1980s pop/bubblegum with the stripped down and sometimes simplistic grooves of kwaito music. 'We had joined Cool Spot as engineers for people who were there to make demos, it was just us having fun and messing around in the studio to try something different,' says Spikiri.

There was a moment at the SAMAs two years ago that I will never forget. In the weeks leading up to the event, which was held as always at the Sun City Superbowl, there had been an announcement that the Port Elizabeth-born high priest of South African jazz, Zim Ngqawana, would be receiving a lifetime achievement award. Along with him, Mdu and Spikiri would also be honoured for their many contributions to South African music.

The optimist in me, the one who'd been raised as Catholic and was enchanted with the redeeming powers of a good story and a happy ending, started to get hopeful. A little too hopeful. I badly wanted to believe that Mdu and Spikiri would take this moment, at the tail-end of their careers, to relive a bygone era and perform together on a big stage and to, if only for a fleeting moment, show us what would have been possible had MM Deluxe not broken up. I imagined they would offer a set of three to four songs from each of their varied careers, a medley through time that would perhaps see *Fokol*, Spikiri's anti-anthem for gatecrashers, blending into Mdu's *Mazola*, a declaration that 'si ka daar' (we're over there) and

PRODUCERS PARADISE: A PAEAN FOR THE MEN ON THE BOARDS

'siyangena' (we're coming in).

Or perhaps Spikiri would come out from below the stage with a fiery rendition of *Zodwa*, asking 'ujolanoban?', which would be the perfect setup for Mdu to come in thudding with 'ok'salayo s'yajola'. The connections would be poetic and the possibilities, it seemed, endless. I hoped that, as older men, they would close tabs on all their unresolved chapters and finally embrace each other in a meaningful and public way. But life, in spite of our kwaito fantasies, has a tendency of charting its own course. That night, Mdu and Spikiri didn't perform together. Instead, the focus was on who would take top honours between K.O, Cassper Nyovest and AKA, in what had been a flagship year for South African hip hop.

This is the moment I am thinking about as we drive into the suburb of Gallo Manor on the north side of Joburg. We are a long way away from Ndofaya (Meadowlands), that's for sure. Here we pass a security gate, which is strangely not secure at all. They simply ask us where we are going, we tell them Kalawa and they wave us through. No search of what's in the boot of our car, no credentials asked for or anything. One should be grateful, but at that moment all I can ask myself is what was the point of all that then, the boom gate and the security detail?

As we drive into a small gated house just on the pivot of a corner joining two streets, you can hear small thuds of drum and bass at work on the other end of the building. This place isn't what you think about when you think of Kalawa. One might be inclined to think of street bashes, spinning cars and gun-toting pantsulas in multi-coloured overalls. The reality is much more underwhelming: a peach-coloured house with a brick driveway. There are leaves all over the place and inside, a kitchen that looks abandoned. Another room seems to be an office, and from the window I can make out lever-arch files with each of the members of Trompies's names on them. The files are bulging with paperwork and sit facing an empty swivel chair. Outside, there's a small bench where we decide to perch. Spikiri, wearing black pants, a navy t-shirt, a King Don Father chain and sporting amagoda, comes out to meet us. We exchange greetings, and Spikiri also greets Esi, who is sitting in the backseat of our transport. He then has a brief convo with Lance Stehr, who is our lift here, about not having seen each other in a long time.

What surprises me is how short Spikiri is. I guess because of the way he is always framed in his videos and on album covers, coupled with the fact that he idolises the very tall Snoop Dogg, I had always associated Spikiri with height. In reality he's a small guy, with a slight frame, but he still has big presence. His voice is somewhere between raspy and tired. Shy and reclusive, when he speaks he fiddles with his fingers and hands. I study them closely, longish fingers slightly ashy on the edges, but really well manicured. These are the hands that have orchestrated two decades worth of hits. He talks in that hoarse, lazy voice of his:

> In South African people don't recognise you whilst you are still alive unless they feel like you've really made a contribution. I mean, I just got three lifetime achievement awards. That is a top honour, and it makes me feel good to know that something I have done is so appreciated. You must be able to deal with different people's styles. I mean, here at Kalawa you have Bongo Maffin which is more of an afro-pop vibe, you have Trompies which is, like, hardcore kwaito, or a Busiswa who is more up-tempo house; so always as a producer you must be versatile.

Spikiri doesn't have a lot time on his hands these days. He is putting on the final spices on a landmark album. Entitled *The King Don Father*, his latest record is a celebration of a life lived in music. From where we are sitting, we can hear the beats on loop that he is busy cooking up in his dark and surprisingly simple studio. The boys from Uhuru are in studio with him today and keep working whilst we sit outside shooting the breeze. He's been refining this project for a while, he says. 'I can take a year making one song. That's how professional I am, because when it's out there you can't take it back. I've been working on this album for three years now, and it's only about to come out now, and I'm happy,' he says. I believe him.

But before all that, I ask him to take us back to the beginning. It has taken Spikiri a lot to get here. 'This industry is small and I've always known that. So I've tried not to just think of myself, because we need each other. You must always be open,' he says. What makes Spikiri one of the best producers this country will ever have is his unrelenting sense of curiosity. It was this desire to know more that lead Spikiri out of the humdrum of small-scale bands and into the classrooms of FUBA, which was then one of the premier music schools in the country. Speaking about his time there, Spikiri recalls being enchanted by having the space and freedom to study music all day. 'It was nice. We had our own band, and that is where I really started composing my own music. But I didn't stay there for a long time because I wanted to start making music.'

Spikiri attended FUBA just a few years before the school's greatest student, Moses Taiwa Molelekwa, would walk the campus lawns. Spikiri, however, recalls the likes of Saleolo Selota being among his schoolmates. He says FUBA is the first place where he really learned one of the most important weapons in his arsenal: how to collaborate.

I learned a lot about instrumentation, and my advantage is that because I can play my own instruments I don't depend on anyone. So that also makes me versatile and I can work with anyone. I am not just a writer of songs. If someone comes in the studio and asks for a song, I can say okay let's go ahead and do it. I have all the skills I need. I don't have to wait for anyone.

Where Were You? Is the first foray Spikiri made in his own right into the music scene, coming together with Mdu Masilela as MM Deluxe. It's a unique kind of late 1980s album in that it is not as 'confrontational' as records of that era tended to be. Instead, it's a record that hangs its hat almost entirely on being soulful. At times deliberately all over the place, the album is the result of the serious dabbler and the serious connoisseur blending into a beautiful synthesis. The title track, *New Generation* and also *Angerous*, are particular standout joints. Full of raw power and flashes of unfiltered emotion, *Where Were You?* was the perfect foretaste of the political innuendos, youthful provocations and tough-guy lifestyle in songs that would become the bedrock of kwaito half a decade later.

Where Were You? may be the album of note when you talk about MM Deluxe, but what is lesser known is that it isn't the only album by the duo. In 1990 they released their sophomore project *Be Free My People*. The project sees MM Deluxe go deeper into the wilderness of funk. With cuts like *There's No Stopping Us* and *Putsu Putsu*, *Be Free My People* is a much more preppy undertaking. It is an album about the construction of identity through memory in service of communal agendas. It is the kind of thing that forces you to let go of choreographed emotions and gives you permission to feel, and especially, to feel good.

Shortly after the release of *Be Free My People* however, MM Deluxe decided to call it quits. According to Spikiri, the decision for MM Deluxe to go their separate ways was both mutual and gradual. 'Mdu started working for another company and I started working for another company, so it wasn't that we weren't friends anymore. We just didn't have the time to dedicate to making more music together.'

When the duo went their separate ways, at least in the immediate term, Mdu became the bigger star. He was courted by countless record labels and given the autonomy to make whatever music he wanted, as well as carte blanche over how to roll out distribution. But like many kwaito record labels of the era, Mdu's record label was a one-man show. Despite having a keen ear for music and

PRODUCERS PARADISE: A PAEAN FOR THE MEN ON THE BOARDS

the ability to craft vast, complex sonic landscapes, his vision was limited by his commitments as a solo artist.

At the height of his popularity Mdu tells me he would do up to eight shows a week, often driving long distances to and from venues. This meant that many of his artists, such as his group Mashamplani, and Mawillies, felt abandoned and frustrated. The working relationships became strained. Mdu remembers the time well:

> You have to understand that a lot of us didn't have a template of how to make things work; being a record label owner and being an artist at the same time. You could say we were learning on the job. As a result there were a lot of mistakes that were made, and there was a lot of miscommunication. Plus we were young back then, and that also had a lot to do with not being able to handle things differently.

It was during this time that Spikiri, whose star had waned since his career-altering exit from MM Deluxe, entered a rebuilding phase. He had linked up with lifelong friends Eugene Khoza, Zynne aka 'Mahoota' and Jairus, and they formed Trompies. Mdu is married to Sara, sister to Jairus Nkwe, who is one forth of Trompies, so here the connections ran deeper than just music. Trompies's production company Jazzmee also joined up with Kalawa, which at the time comprised of Oskido, Christos and jazz maestro Don Laka. The joint force, Kalawa Jazzmee, has become an integral part of the local music industry. Spikiri shares the secret to their staying power:

> We've been around for decades now and we've had lots of big artists and sold so many records. We are 100% black owned and that is something special. Most companies start well, but they don't last because when money starts coming in, it becomes a case of 'more money more problems'. This doesn't mean that as Kalawa Jazzmee we don't have our own

problems, but we know how to sit down and solve them. That's why we are still together.

Spikiri confesses that what made Trompies work so hard was a realisation that time was passing them by. By the time the group, which has gone on to define kwaito culture and its visual, fashion and dance aesthetics, was formed, most of its members were already on the brink of their 30s. The reality of music being a young man's game forced them to put in countless hours in studio refining their sound and piling up the tracks so that the gaps between album releases wouldn't stretch too wide. Eugene Khoza, aka 'Donald Duck', had done a stint as a keyboardist for Lucky Dube's backing band, The Slaves, while Mahoota was a trained pianist from the Royal Academy in London, but up until that point nothing had seemed to be working out for them as frontline members of any group.

Spikiri tells me that the name of the group was inspired by a naughty kid on the cartoon programme *Trompie En Die Boksombende*. Although regarded by many as the leader of the group, Spikiri is reluctant to lay claim to that role. He credits everyone equally for the band's success and insists he was cast in the role of leader simply because he had more musical experience than the rest of his brothers-in-arms. He maintains that each member has a specific and important role to play. He expounds further on the group dynamics that have worked so well for Trompies:

> In a group you must have an identity. Even if there are five of you on a song, when you come in you need to sound different. People must know who this is now, so you have to be original and inventive. Most of the other kwaito groups haven't lasted because once one of you says, 'I'm the boss', there's going to be some serious problems. In Trompies we are equal and it doesn't matter that I can produce more or that Jairus can write better. We all contribute something. Even with money, each member gets an equal slice of the pie.

Trompies debuted in 1995 with the album *Shosholoza*, a lean 11-track project that included the anthemic *Sweety Lavo*. To date, that project ranks as one of the standard-bearers in this thing called kwaito. *Shosholoza* was the album where Spikiri would imprint the defining feature of his sound: a thumping bassline that 'swangs'. 'You must have a signature. Even if I am not singing on a song you must hear that this is Spikiri's work. I don't mess around when it comes to protecting my legacy. That baseline is my signature,' he says insistently.

Trompies seemed to walk into the perfect storm of supergroups. Around that time Boom Shaka was blowing up, and TKZee were also simmering. Bongo Maffin's 'chimurenga rave' signature sound was the talk of the town, and Alaska were the kings of the township. Abashante weren't too far off the centre either. Spikiri explains that it became on obsession of theirs to distinguish themselves:

Our biggest problem as black South Africans is that we don't believe in ourselves. That's why I love Nigerians, because they believe in themselves. As for me, I don't wanna follow nobody. I want to be followed. That's what has made this company, Kalawa Jazzmee, so big. It's because everything we do is authentic. You must have a unique identity which sets you apart.

Trompies incorporated pantsula dance culture into their identity from the get-go. Their synchronised dance numbers and street codes were a distinguishing signifier. Spikiri explains the philosophy behind his contribution to the group's choices:

Ghetto was something integral to me. I'm kwaito. I'm from the ghetto and I grew up as a pantsula. That's how people know me. You know, pantsulas are always happy and hyper people. And I'm not flashy. I like to keep it simple. I don't want to alienate the people I hang out with. I want people, when they are with me, to feel comfortable. I don't want them to feel like they are low class.

There's no doubt about Spikiri's street credentials, and I know better than to question them. Instead I ask him, if he's been ghetto all his life, what is he doing here in the suburbs?

Well in the townships you will never know peace, truly speaking. It's nice when you visit. I go to the township, but when I need to rest my head I come back here. You see, sometimes in the township people are always expecting you to have money. I try to avoid those things. I have lived ekasi and I know the streets, but being in the suburbs doesn't mean you forget the people you came up with.

Trompies's catalogue is the most imaginative in all of kwaito. It is a pledge to living your best life. Moody and evocative, Trompies have a knack for creating songs that attach themselves to our memories. I can never seem to erase the picture of my junior primary girlfriend, Nomcebo Ndlovu, dancing to *Magasman* at a school end-of-term dance. I remember I was leaning against one of the pillars in the hall as Lebo Mathosa made soulful threats and recited the names of the Trompies band members on the hook. 'Gene, Mandla, Zynne, Jairus', and all I can remember is watching my girlfriend dance and thinking this was the most beautiful girl in the world. Thinking that we would be in love forever...

Despite the baggage that people like me tend to attach to his music, Spikiri is surprisingly free of nostalgia about his own work. Instead, 'forward' is clearly the battle cry and focus of this kwaito legend. Perhaps it is this lack of sentimentality that has enabled him to be a sure thing for at least 25 years. These days, he spends his hours making club bangers for Professor, Busiswa and Uhuru, and he shows no signs of slowing down. Keeping it simple is part of his approach, he says.

Our fans are very sensitive. If you keep on jumping between sounds you can lose people easily, because they won't know or understand what's going on with your sound. Even if they supported you before, you could find you have to start afresh and build a new fan base. At the same time, you have to mature with your audience. You have to show growth. Every time I produce, I want to produce something that will last forever.

Nobody remembers us

If I'd known this would be Robbie Malinga's last interview I would have asked better questions. Perhaps something about working with Doc Shebeleza and his studio habits. Maybe a question about the architecture of the vocals on Brown Dash's albums, or perhaps a few mentions about the links between kwaito and afrobeat. Instead, for the 20 minutes we were on the phone, three days before he passed away, Robbie and I were talking about a small confrontation that happened at a Mabala Noise concert a few months earlier. Let me lay it down for you so you can get familiar.

The radio station that butters my bread had given me VIP tickets to the Durban July Mabala Noise concert, where over 30 artists were supposed to perform. Of course, after noise disturbance complaints and with the show swinging beyond the early hours of the morning, not even half the scheduled bill had taken to the stage before the show was shut down. But before the cops came knocking, I had made my way past a maze of tipsy teens excited to see their idols perform and towards the gate (I had to give entry tickets to my spouse). As I waited there, Robbie and the new afro-soul crooner, Musa, were coming in, and there was an exchange of words as Robbie didn't want to be padded down and searched by security at the gate. 'Security guards get too familiar sometimes,' he jokingly tells me. 'When they see that you are someone with a name, they want to use that to get attention. So they get extra spicy to show you they are in charge.'

Robbie has been around long enough to have had to deal with enough spicy security guards in his time. I also imagine that most of the security guards get so spicy because they actually don't know who Robbie Malinga is. Well maybe they do now, perhaps familiar with him from his multiple afro-pop hits and ballad collaborations with the likes of Musa, Kelly Khumalo, Zahara and Naima Kay. 'They think I'm just the guy who makes soppy love songs so I won't tell them off,' he says, before breaking into uproarious laughter.

What you might not know, like those security guards, is that before Robbie Malinga rebranded himself as an afro-pop sensation with a knack for making hit duet songs, he was at the forefront of shaping the sound of kwaito. He helped pioneer a strain of the music, whose defining characteristic was layered harmonies and synthesised grooves that landed on the offbeat. It was a sound that dominated the late nineties and early 2000s and is a period far too little spoken about in music today. Robbie reflects on the subtle shift he was at the centre of:

> What most people don't get about the sound of kwaito is that, at first, it was music about celebrating this freedom that we'd just got, and so we made a lot of party songs. But you can only party for so long. Soon we realized that not everything was all balloons and firecrackers. Yes we'd voted, but what did that all mean? So you had this transition into a more reflective storytelling around 1999, when Mbeki came to power, because now people were starting to ask questions. What does it mean to vote and yet I have no house or job? What does it mean that my uncle who fought in the struggle now has to hijack cars? What does it mean that I have AIDS and no access to medicine? We tried to be poetic about it, but all of it was there. A restlessness.

PRODUCERS PARADISE: A PAEAN FOR THE MEN ON THE BOARDS

Robbie Malinga has a deadpan humour. The kind of guy who likes to make a very valid point and then immediately make fun of the kind of people, people like him, who say what he has just said. Humour in serious times is also an important part of Robbie Malinga's version of kwaito. Instead of chasing anthems, they somehow seem to have come chasing after him. Robbie made music with a lo-fi DIY aesthetic. Music that stripped away at the praise of violence, which was commonplace in the genre, and confronted communities in mourning in a subtle and nonchalant manner. On his approach to songwriting he says:

> Music must never sound like it has an agenda. Whichever way you structure the song, or in whatever you write, you must think about what you want to express yes, but also be clear about what you want your audience to receive and how. Because you might listen to a song whose message you agree with, but if the artist seems like they are forcing an agenda on you and not allowing you to make up your own mind, then it's a turn-off.

Robbie Malinga knows his audience. A driving theme in songs he has written and produced is the artist's desire to succeed, to make it to the top, to have excessive amounts of money and watch the shiny faces of his admirers in the front row as they scream his name. In the last few years of his life Robbie Malinga had both, and he was trying his best not to squander them.

> I think as producers nobody really speaks to us about finances, especially when you are young and coming into the industry. One of my biggest regrets is that when we were starting out we spent money recklessly because it seemed to come so easy. Then you die broke, as we've seen with so many people in the industry, and everybody wonders what happened. Nobody remembers us producers.

A few days later, fresh with the information that Robbie Malinga is dead at 47, I listen back to the tape of our conversation, and that is the phrase that sticks out: 'Nobody remembers us'. Here is the thing about producers: they see themselves as part of a single tribe, working in the darkness to bring the music to light. Often this means nobody sees them, but it benefits one a great deal to seek them out and find their brand of redemption on the dance floor. So I won't end this with some anecdote about Robbie Malinga, his prowess on the ones and twos, or a funny story about recording with a high Brown Dash that is best left unshared. Instead, I will tell you a few things about Robbie and his tribe.

Don't try and take Guffy on. On those lower registers, you're gonna lose every time. Nobody shreds a kwaito guitar like Gabi le Roux. Let D-rex be D-rex and everything will fall into place. Last night Spikiri's bassline saved my life. Mdu was leaving hits on the cutting room floor since before your mama was letting you come outside. Zwai Bala is a national key point. Protect him at all costs. Let the record show I have a signed copy of Kaybee's sessions in the house I grew up in, and I'm keeping that for my son. Any slander of DJ Cleo's name is retired with immediate effect. Oskido might infuriate me sometimes, but I'm so glad he is around. Somebody should get Tronix on the phone and tell him I said thank you for everything. We lost Kyllex too soon. Khabzela too. What Robbie Malinga did for us, no one can undo.

XV

Looking back to the future
Esinako Ndabeni

In 2017, Kwesta released the song *Spirit,* which featured the Nigerian-American rapper Wale. Makwa, the producer of this hit record, which has since gone triple platinum, had sampled Spiritchaser's *These Tears* and slowed it down. The song, opening with the words 'Zimb' indaba' and sung in isiZulu by Kwesta, was reminiscent of the production of old school kwaito music: a sample, a slowed down house track and some lyrics in a vernacular language. *Spirit* sounds like a dark room filled with carefree black people doing the get-down with bottles of Savannah and Black Label in their hands. In short, it sounds like kwaito. I had not been writing for a while when I heard the song. That moment made me feel as though kwaito had come out of hiding, and it was going to take the mainstream music scene by storm again.

Riky Rick, another hip hop artist, had released his kwaito-inspired single *Stay Shining,* featuring Cassper Nyovest, Professor, Major League and Ali Keys. I started writing again, confident that a movement of modern kwaito that was still true to the old-school kwaito would begin. After all, South African hip hop artists had flirted with kwaito in the past. K.O and Kid X's *Caracara* had sampled Trompies's *Bengimngaka* and even made references to TKZee's *Dlala Mapantsula*. AKA and K.O had sampled TKZee's *Nkosi Sikelela* on their hit song *Run Jozi*.

South Africa's current crop of hip hop artists have been unafraid to communicate their appreciation for the kwaito generation; a refreshing perspective on kwaito, seeing there had been a tension between kwaito and hip hop in the years of kwaito's reign. So, when a hip hop artist like Kwesta made a kwaito song years after the kwaito revolution, it made me think that maybe kwaito could re-enter the mainstream if a more current approach to the production was used.

But my excitement dwindled after a while, as no further developments came through. What I thought marked a turning point didn't gain any momentum. So we kwaito enthusiasts had to return to our Trompies, Boom Shaka, Mandoza and others for our supply. To my mind, the one song that marks the transition away from kwaito's reign is Big Nuz's *Umlilo*. While the 2009 release felt like a continuation of the genre, it marked an era where the focus in mainstream music shifted away from kwaito as we knew it. It seemed that this was something that Big Nuz was aware of as well, as the song's video featured a group of people carrying placards with the words, 'Where is kwaito?', 'Kwaito must die', 'Kwaito is dead' and 'Who is Big Nuz?'.

South Africa's entertainment industry often tells the story of a fall from grace for many of its artists. And indeed, many kwaito artists have not been able to transition into the post-kwaito entertainment industry. We speak of many of them, even though they are by no means old, in the past tense. This is why Kalawa Jazmee, led by Spikiri, Oskido, Bruce Sebitlo and Don Laka, has been so remarkable in its ability to remain at the forefront of South Africa's seemingly fickle music industry.

Deciding which tense to use to discuss kwaito has been my struggle throughout this book. Many have let go. Kwaito is dead, they say. It *was* great, and now it's just a throwback. However, some of us, like Spikiri, do not believe that kwaito music can die. Kwaito *is* a genre that characterises the black South African experience. Beyond the music, these people perceive kwaito to be a movement; an embodiment of identity. This much is true: kwaito is alive in people's hearts. And we still attach so much of how our identity has been shaped to the kwaito movement.

I remember attending Head Honcho's Stay Fresh event in 2017. TKZee were billed to perform, and I could not afford to go. On that day I camped on Head Honcho's Twitter page, asking them what they wanted me to do to see my favorite kwaito group for free. At the time, I had a blog called *DON'T CALL ME KAFFIR* which was dedicated to my love for kwaito and its politics. A few of my followers rallied behind me to get me the tickets, because we all imagined that I loved kwaito the most out of all my peers. Head Honcho was kind enough to give into my nagging, and that's how my best friend and I ended up on the VIP guest list for the event.

When the time came for TKZee to perform, there was almost a stampede and some tension as people (me) passively-aggressively tried to get ahead of others in attendance, the better to watch this group from the front row. I knew that TKZee was forever, but I did not know that this feeling was one that resonated with so many among my generation. It would be worthwhile for me to mention here that I had only been alive for a year when TKZee's debut album, *Halloween*, was released. This was in 1998. It is undeniable that during kwaito's reign I was too young to understand the significance of the genre and to link the musical experience to the Black South African experience.

However, 19 years later, with a 20-year-old me at a hip hop event, it became clear that my generation had kept kwaito alive in our hearts and in our homes; that our most precious recollections of childhood were attached to the kwaito soundtrack. It was an awakening for me as we all excitedly sang TKZee's music back to them word-for-word at this event that was mostly attended by middle-class youths, or at least youths who move comfortably in middle-class spaces. And, ultimately, that is one of many things that kwaito is; it is the soundtrack to a complicated childhood. I cannot hear Brown Dash's *Phants' Komthunz' Welanga* without thinking about the childhood games that I would play with my friends in Waterfall, Mthatha when we were kids. 'Ndazibeka, ndazincothula'; where we had to say 'Ndazibeka' (I have placed myself) when we sat down and 'Ndazincothula' (I have picked myself up) when we stood up, or we would be slapped by the person with whom we were playing. 'Xhwips'; where we had to remember to say, 'niks xhwips', so that the person we were playing with would not snatch (xhwips) our food from us. Dushe: a game of 'duck' that we played with balls made out of plastic bags from Boxer, Shoprite and Spar.

Mzekezeke's *Guqa Ngamadolo* is forever the soundtrack to the time when our neighbours with dogs would pour water into plastic bottles and leave these bottles on the grass to scare the dogs away from peeing on the grass. There are many experiences that I have lived through the lens of kwaito music. Childhood, something that already has a lot of nostalgia attached to it because of its innocence, becomes something that is even more special when I remember that I got to be a child at a time when kwaito was dominating the mainstream. I remember us as we stood in front our parents and their friends, tapping our heads with rhythm as we did the choreography to Mshoza and Mzambiya's *Kortes* for them, to their great amusement.

We are a people characterised by mobility; from rags to Edgars accounts, and kwaito is also the soundtrack to some darkness in my life. It is the soundtrack to little me, my grandfather and my aunt being evicted from our one-roomed home in Waterfall where my aunt and I slept on a mattress on the floor. It is the soundtrack to having to live at the school where my grandfather drove the school bus. It is the soundtrack to those nights my aunt and I spent stealing peanut butter from the school because it was a luxury for us at that time.

Kwaito is the soundtrack to my grandfather and I driving past our mud home in Mandela as the winds blew it down one rainy day, and knowing we would have to move back to our rural home. Whenever Makhendlas's *Iminwe* would play, my family would remind me about my late uncle Thamsanqa who died in 1998, and how the two of us would sing the song to each other. I have no recollection of this, but to this day *Iminwe* is mine and my uncle's song. Kwaito represents even the experiences that have escaped my memory.

The more conversations I have with my black friends, the ones who have also moved out of poverty and now occupy middle-class positions in society, the clearer it becomes that our lives mirror the journey that kwaito has taken; letting go, being hopeful, being dispossessed, and moving up. And for all these experiences I attach to the music, for all the optimism that many have and the rigour with which we approach living, it is also clear that kwaito music does not hold the power that it once did. Even those among its pioneers who have remained relevant have moved on to produce music in other genres.

But all is not lost. We have gqom now.

Yile gqomu

While Durban kwaito has held the South African music industry down for years, gqom has emerged as a sound that can rival the size of what the kwaito industry used to be. Quick to notice this, Afrotainment and Kalawa Jazmee have ensured that this is a movement they become a part of. A reaction to house and electro music, gqom started when artists from the Eastern Cape and Kwa-Zulu-Natal made these dark, repetitive, fast-paced house beats with synths off Fruityloops software.

The sound of gqom was not one that was foreign to my ears. Growing up in the Eastern Cape, I had also grown up to music that sounded a great deal like igqomu. At the time, this sound was known as 'isjokojoko', a noisy version of house music characterised by the same repetitiveness that one hears in gqom. It was audible in the isjokojoko songs that this was not music which required much of a budget, with cheap equipment being used, and the same is also true for the roots of igqomu. The major difference, however, would be that isjokojoko employed more words than the average gqom song; often crude lyrical content about having or desiring sex. Isjokojoko came into our lives through DJ Mthura's *Ndingalwa Ndibebomvu*, and DJ Soso had a series of hits such as *Iharika* and *Ntombazana Qoshela*.

The perception persists among many people that igqomu has its roots in the Eastern Cape. Whatever the case will turn out to be, igqomu has emerged into full popularity from KwaZulu-Natal, with most of its music sung in isiZulu. Igqomu, an onomatopoeiac word for the sound that the drum makes, is a sound that appeals to the young black South African's instinct for dance. Like kwaito, it is a sound that has emerged out of township night life, and has therefore been met with skepticism and dismissed as mere 'noise' by many.

However, as we grow and begin to understand that our senses of identity do not have to be confined to one narrative, the youth have found a way to understand that we can be fully involved in other musical genres while also showing support and a desire for gqom to succeed in the mainstream.

When the DJ duo Distruction Boyz released their album *Gqom Is The Future* in 2017, they pleaded with their fans to help the album reach gold status, as no other gqom album had achieved that. Indeed, under the hashtag #DistructionBoyzGoesGold, the album became the first gqom album to reach gold status, selling over 15 000 album copies with the help of social media. To further cement the impact that gqom has had, the single *Omunye* from that album was voted SAMA Song of the Year in 2017, another new milestone for gqom.

LOOKING BACK TO THE FUTURE

Going even further than kwaito, the gqom wave has now hit the international community. I was excited to hear Babes Wodumo's *Wololo* on the *Black Panther* movie soundtrack. Since then, we have seen a great deal of people from the international community uploading videos of themselves dancing to gqom music onto social media. I, for one, did not imagine that this genre would live long or gain traction in the international community. I confess, I imagined that it was the new kwaito, and bound to die in the same way.

So much more than party music, kwaito created cultural and economic opportunity for South Africa's black youth. I must allow myself to move on now. Kwaito will live on for far longer than I or this book will because it is an identity, a loaded history with profound reflections on the life of every day South Africans in post-apartheid South Africa. So now, I will take lessons from the kwaito generation into my generation and beyond.

About the Authors

ESINAKO NDABENI is currently pursuing her degree in international relations and anthropology at the University of Cape Town. She intends on studying anthropology in postgraduate studies with a specific focus on popular culture in South Africa, along with its socio-political importance. She is the founder of the blog *DON'T CALL ME KAFFIR* – a blog which has primarily been an attempt at bringing kwaito music [back] into the forefront of black discourse on blackness. This will be her debut book.

SIHLE MTHEMBU is an award-winning journalist and filmmaker born in Mooi River in the Natal Midlands. In 2009 Mthembu enrolled in the Durban University of Technology where he graduated with a BTech in journalism. He has worked as an art critic, a business journalist and a churner of various types of online banter.

REFERENCES

Readings

Ansel, G (2014) Brenda Fassie: The Gender Context, *The Con Mag* [Online] http://www.theconmag.co.za/2014/06/26/brenda-fassie-the-gender-context/.

Blose, M (2012) Pornographic Objectification of Women through Kwaito Lyrics, *Agenda*, **26** (3) pp 50–60

Bogatsu, M (2002) 'Loxion Kulcha': Fashioning Black Youth Culture in Post-Apartheid South Africa, *English Studies in Africa*, **45** (2) [Online] https://www.tandfonline.com/doi/abs/10.1080/00138390208691311

Boloka, G (2003) Cultural Studies and the Transformation of the Music Industry: Some reflections on kwaito, in *Shifting Selves: Post-Apartheid Essays on Mass Media, Culture, and Identity*, ed H Wasserman and S Jacobs, Kwela Books, Cape Town

Bynoe, Y (2002) Getting Real about Global Hip Hop, *Georgetown Journal of International Affairs*, **3** (1), pp 78–84 [Online] https://www.jstor.org/stable/43133478?seq=1#page_scan_tab_contents

Davids, A (1990) The 'Coloured' Image of Afrikaans in Nineteenth Century Cape Town, *Kronos*, pp 36–47 [Online] www.jstor.org/stable/41056280

Deumert, A, Tsotsitaal Online – The Creativity of Tradition in *Analyzing Multilingual Youth Practices in Computer in Computer Mediated Communication (CMC)* ed C Cutler and U Royneland [Online] https://www.academia.edu/23416645/Tsotsitaal_Online_The_Creativity_of_Tradition_1?auto=download

Haupt, A (2008) Black Masculinity and the Tyranny of Authenticity in South African Popular Culture in *Power, Politics and Identity in South African Media: Selected seminar papers*, ed A Hadland, pp 378–398, Cape Town, HSRC Press

Hurst, E (2009) Tsotsitaal, Global Culture and Local Style: Identity and recontextualisation in twenty-first century South African townships, *Social Dynamics: A Journal of African Studies,* **35** (2) pp 244–257

Impey, A (2001) Resurrecting the Flesh? Reflections on women in kwaito, *Agenda*, **16** (49) pp 44–50

Jappie, S (2015) Writing the City in a Different Script, *Chimurenga Chronic* [Online] http://chimurengachronic.co.za/writing-the-city-in-a-different-script/

Makhoba, N (2018) Chicco Twala: Brenda Fassie is mine, *The City Press* [Online] https://www.channel24.co.za/Movies/News/chicco-twala-brenda-fassie-is-mine-20180114

Mahali, A (2016) Maid to Serve: 'Self-Fashioning' and the Domestic Worker Trope, *Journal of African Media Studies*, **8** (2) pp 127–143 [Online] https://www.ingentaconnect/2016/00000008/00000002/art00002

Motloi, M (2007) *Kwaito Music: A Cultural Revolution*, Ratsosa Publishing, Pretoria

Ntshangase, D (1995) Indaba yami i-straight: Language and language practices in Soweto in *Language and Social History: Studies in South African Sociolinguistics*, ed R Mesthrie, pp 291

Ntombela, S (2012) Do Clothes Make a (Wo)man? Exploring the role of dress in shaping South African domestic workers' identities, in *Was it something I wore?: Dress, identity, materiality*, HSRC Press, Cape Town, pp 132–147

Nyamnjoh, F (2015) Incompleteness: Frontier Africa and the Currency of Conviviality, *Journal of Asian and African Studies*, **52** (3), pp 253–270

Peterson, B (2003) Kwaito, 'Dawgs' and the Antimonies of Hustling, *African Identities Journal*, pp 197–213 [Online] https://www.tandfonline.com/doi/fu

REFERENCES

ll/10.1080/1472584032000175650

Olifant, N. 2012. *Musos to hit political decks*. IOL News. [Online] https://www.iol.co.za/entertainment/celebrity-news/local/musos-to-hit-political-decks-1446106

Slabbert, S and Myers-Scotton, C, *The structure of Tsotsitaal and Iscamtho: Code Switching and in-group Identity in South African Townships* [Online] https://www.academia.edu/82499/The_structure_of_Tsotsitaal_and_in-group_identity_inSouth_African_townships

Steingo, G (2007) The Politicization of 'Kwaito': From the 'Party Politic' to 'Party Politics.', *Black Music Research Journal*, **27** (1) pp 23–44 [Online] http://www.jstor.org/stable/25433779?seq=1#page_scan_tab_contents.

Steingo, G (2008) Historicizing Kwaito, *International Library of African Music*, **8** (2) pp 76-91 [Online] http://www.jstor.org/stable/30250016

Steingo, G (2008) Producing Kwaito: 'Nkosi Sikelel' iAfrika' After Apartheid, *The World of Music*

Swartz, S (2008) Is kwaito South African hip-hop? Why the answer matters and who it matters to, *The World of Music*, **50** (2) [Online] http://www.jstor.org/stable/41699825?seq=1#page_scan_tab_contents

Films

After Robot: Kwaito Music in Johannesburg, documentary produced by S Klose, Johannesburg, 2002

Afrikaaps, documentary by D Valley, Cape Town, 2010

Gqom Wave, documentary by DJ Maphorisa, 2017

Taking Kwaito International, TEDx talk by Ees, Muenster, 2013

Magazine Archives

DRUM Magazine

Y Magazine